P9-DUJ-492

WORLD OF CULTURE

MUSIC

by Frederic V. Grunfeld

Newsweek Books, New York

NEWSWEEK BOOKS

Joseph L. Gardner, Editor

Janet Czarnetzki, Art Director
Edwin D. Bayrd, Jr., Associate Editor
Ellen Kavier, Researcher-Writer
Elaine Andrews, Copy Editor

S. Arthur Dembner, President

ARNOLDO MONDADORI EDITORE

Giuliana Nannicini, Editor

Mariella De Battisti, Picture Researcher
Marisa Melis, Editorial Secretary
Enrico Segré, Designer
Giovanni Adamoli, Production Coordinator

Contents

1

The Family of Music

WHEN A MODERN MINSTREL like Paul McCartney picks up his electric guitar, steps to the microphone, and sings "My Love," he is adding yet another link to a chain of musical tradition that stretches back to the dawn of mankind. The guitar he holds in his hands is the latest mutation of an instrument whose shape can be seen on 3,000-year-old Hittite bas-reliefs and whose name goes back to a still older Middle Eastern word, *si-tar*—"three strings"—which indicates that other strings have been added at later stages of its evolution into the "Spanish guitar" and thence into the mainstay of blues and pop music.

The melody McCartney sings contains reminiscences of both African and European folksongs. It owes its lithe, elastic shape partly to the African-descended blues and partly to English and Scotch-Irish ballads that reveal their age by using ancient five-note scales or the Dorian and Aeolian modes of the Middle Ages. The underlying beat of the rhythm has come out of Africa, a continent preeminent in matters of the drum and the dance, although it has lost most of its African subtleties in the process of being adapted to a ballad beat. The chords with which he harmonizes his melody are a specifically European contribution to this alloy. They had to undergo an elaborate evolution at the courts of Burgundy, in Johann Sebastian Bach's organ loft, and in George Gershwin's Tin Pan Alley before arriving at their present state.

As for the words, they too belong to a great tradition, and it is not difficult to find comparable examples in every part of the world, whether among the Berbers of North Africa,

> Do not trample down the furrows, little gazelle.
> I am ready now to show you
> The path that you do not know.

or the headhunters of Borneo,

> The seashell is transparent,
> The banana is good to eat.
> You are beautiful, girl!
> And your breasts are still soft.

or among the Eskimos of Greenland,

> My betrothed, my beloved,
> I leave you now.
> Do not sorrow too much for me.
> I cannot forget you . . .

The Baulé tribesmen of Africa's Ivory Coast still play the simple instruments of their remote forebears, thus perpetuating a form of musicmaking that is millennia old. African rhythms have been a major influence on modern music.

7

All who love one another
Find it hard to part . . .

The musical means that are used to express these sentiments vary enormously from Greenland to Tierra del Fuego. But the basic kinetic and emotional impulse is the same, and the acoustical laws that govern their expression are immutable. In that sense, music is, if not a universal language, at least a universal means of communication between human beings. And it is not only the love song that is ubiquitous, but also the work song. The fishermen of Greece, the sailors of Japan, the Maoris of New Zealand, and the men who ply the Nile and Brahmaputra rivers all have their boat songs. A Navajo Indian silversmith sings in rhythm to the tap-tap of his hammer; a Spanish olive farmer, riding to his orchard in Andalusia, sings a long, mellow chant in rhythm to the hoofbeats of his mule–a song that floats out over the surrounding countryside like smoke rising and curling on a breeze.

In the cities of the industrial world, the rise of the discothèque, taking over from the far more pretentious night club, has restored the dance to at least a vestige of its ancient place at the center of tribal social life. As an arena in which to unleash one's dance instincts, a discothèque floor is not so different from a jungle clearing, and the rites that are performed in both places serve very much the same function. Once, in the jungles of Orissa in central India, I observed a dance on a full-moon night when a whole village of naked aborigines of the Saora tribe had worked themselves up to a frenzied dance pitch. Then the drums began beating, and the young women turned up en masse and formed a long row, linking arms, their breasts bobbing jauntily as they surged backward and forward, while the young men pranced wildly in

Stringed instruments, creations of infinite variety and almost universal appeal, represent a major advance over the simple resonating chambers of early neolithic times. Primitive harps such as the Mesopotamian model featured on the terra-cotta relief at right were the forerunners of more refined stringed instruments. Among the latter are, from left to right below: an Abyssinian lyre, an Arabian rebab, an Indian sarangi carved from a single piece of wood, a sinuous Russian guitar, a double-keyboard guitar, and a classic Spanish guitar.

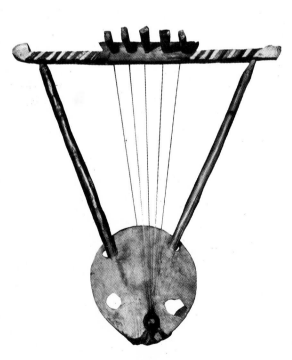

front of them, beating all sorts of percussion instruments and letting out blood-curdling cries of sheer happiness. Only after everyone had reached a state of near exhaustion, what with all the laughing and wriggling and the brandishing of spears and sticks, did the two groups finally merge and the dancers wander off into the night in convenient couples.

On the walls of their adobe huts, the Saora tribesmen paint pictures of these dance sessions that illustrate their importance in the tribal scheme of things. In a flat, fluent style that resembles prehistoric cave painting, they depict the highlight of the festival—a dozen women dancing with linked arms, shoulder to shoulder, so that the smallest ones are left kicking the air because their legs are not long enough to reach the ground. These pictures are not unlike the dance figures that occur in the caves of southern Europe—some of them dating back to the ice age—except that these dancers are usually dressed in animal skins, and their function seems to have been to impersonate wild animals in the dance, to give the hunter magic powers over his prey.

Paintings of this sort furnish the earliest evidence of human musical activity. In southern France, for example, in the cave of Trois Frères in Ariège, there is a rude drawing of a man impersonating a bison, and in his mouth he holds a musical bow—an instrument he supports with his left hand and twangs with his right. The painting is thought to be seventeen thousand years old. Yet this same instrument, essentially a one-string "guitar" using the mouth and skull as sounding board and resonating cavity, can still be heard in some parts of Africa as the "okongo" as well as among the American Indians. It is the original ancestor of all stringed instruments, and its acoustic principles are iden-

tical with those of the other chordophones that can be heard around the world in the form of gourds strung with gut strings, or turtle shells strung with fiber chords, or silken chords mounted on wooden bowls —Persian lutes, Greek lyres, the African kora, the Italian violin, the Indian sitar.

Each of the world's peoples has developed the musical potential of such instruments in its own distinctive fashion. The sitar, for example, has been the king of Indian court music since the fourteenth century, and it, in turn, is a modification of an earlier instrument, the veena (sacred to Saraswathi, the Hindu goddess of art and learning), which has a documented history of some four thousand years. The sitar is made of teak, jackwood (a kind of breadfruit tree), and a seasoned gourd. Its long neck towers above the player's head when he sits cross-legged in the customary playing position. It has six or seven main playing strings running above the frets and, below them, a dozen or so sympathetic strings that set up a steady humming "echo" when the rest are plucked. The sitarist plucks the main strings with a wire plectrum worn on the forefinger of his right hand. Occasionally he reaches out with his little finger and runs it across the sympathetic strings, which give off a sound like a row of broken icicles. Four to twenty arched metal frets are clamped to the neck of the instrument, and these are moved fractionally up or down for each performance, to suit the particular intervals of the raga, or melodic pattern, being played.

The sitar's music is a world in itself, of which most westerners can gain only the most superficial understanding. Learning to play the instrument with any degree of proficiency is a matter of ten or twelve years of intensive study with a guru. Only about ten percent of the music is written down; the vital ninety percent consists of improvisation, when the player can explore an infinite range of melodic possibilities within the strictest limits of tradition. The rhythmic and melodic patterns of Indian music are prescribed by ancient usage and passed

The nobles of ancient Egypt took the music of the harp with them everywhere—even into the Valley of the Dead, the great necropolis at Thebes—as the wall painting at left indicates. In time, the harp's popularity was to decline in the Eastern Mediterranean as public taste shifted to more sophisticated instruments. The ivory detail at right, which once adorned a Mesopotamian casket, shows men playing early versions of the guitar (top) and the recorder (bottom).

from generation to generation via the chain of playing and listening known as *guruparampara*—the all-important master-to-pupil succession that is essential to Indian musical life (and, for that matter, equally important to Polish pianists, or Nigerian drummers, or Japanese koto players; music always has to be learned by hearing someone play it).

To be a sitarist requires both the stamina of an athlete—concerts regularly last into the small hours of the morning—and the spiritual preparation of a monk, for this is an exercise in philosophy as much as in muscular coordination. The raga on which the sitarist decides to improvise must be wholly in harmony with the mood and circumstances of the occasion. And there is a vast range of ragas from which to choose: Kedara, for instance, is meant for "early night, active, confident, joyful and intense"; Kanada is ideal for the "second part of the night, deep happiness and passion"; Hindola is intended for "springtime, bursting life, violence and no softness"; and Megha Mallar is associated with "rainy season, commanding and happy." There are many other possibilities, which Indian artists have depicted in the *raga-mala* ("garland of ragas") paintings, and the number of possible permutations reaches into the hundreds.

During the opening alap ("invocation") of his performance, the sitar player lingers caressingly over each note of the ascending and descending melody—a gradual exposition, full of hesitations and repetitions, that has been compared to the unfolding of a lotus. The tempo speeds up, and the patterns grow more intricate as the tabla drums pick up the thread. The climax is reached anywhere from twenty minutes to two hours later, when the sitarist has accelerated to a dazzling explosion of virtuosity, his fingers flying over frets and strings until the hand is quicker than the ear, and the raga seems to dissolve into a blur of sound.

This highly complex and sophisticated way of organizing the raw material of music is, of course, very different from that of the European tradition. It is a connoisseur's music, although in recent years it has attracted more and more western admirers who are fascinated by the precision and elasticity of the Indian approach. It reflects the historic preference of most of the world's cultures for an elaboration of melody and rhythm, in all of their finest nuances.

Within the worlds of Asian and African music there are, of course, many other equally valid alternatives to the western tradition epitomized by the hundred-man symphony orchestra. The musicians of West Africa form themselves into *ad hoc* orchestras of drums, balaphons, flutes, harps, and miscellaneous percussion instruments that produce a magnificent welter of sounds without requiring written music or rehearsals. Everyone simply knows instinctively and from long experience how to fit his own sounds into the overall pattern. At the same time the dancers move in perfect rhythm to the drums, improvising their steps—shaking, shimmying, with elbows revolving, hips gyrating, heads thrown back, bare heels stamping the ground. And the dancing, like the music, is only a step away from pure acrobatics. I have seen a Senegalese dancer who could turn cartwheels while balancing a glass of water without spilling a drop, and another who could revolve rhythmi-

Using the sitar, an instrument so ancient that its name antedates any known representations of stringed musical devices, Indian musicians created the endlessly improvised raga, a musical pattern with no western equivalent. The Indian dancing girl seen in silhouette above plays a hand drum. In the eighteenth-century miniature at right, a sari-clad woman is shown (lower right) playing an identical drum. Before her sits the ensemble's principal musician, whose veena is a precursor of the modern sitar.

cally atop a free-standing thirty-foot pole, and a third who could do an unconcerned jig on stools while three pairs of assistants twirled ropes over and all around him. The music never seems to stop, for left to itself, a balaphon orchestra may go on all day and all night, and perhaps into the next day, until the last drummer is ready to drop with exhaustion.

The music of Bali suggests another significant alternative to the symphonic way of organizing the tonal substance of music. Virtually the whole island is alive with the music of the percussion groups known as gamelan orchestras. Every village has two or three of them, consisting of twenty or more players presiding over an astonishing assemblage of gongs, drums, and various kinds of metallophones. Some players have only a single note to play; others have a range of three to five notes. They strike their instruments with light wooden hammers in a steady up-down, up-down rhythm that interlocks with, but does not duplicate, that of their neighbors. The result sounds like the jangle of a thousand bells and anvils—organized, however, into very precise rhythmic patterns, sometimes loud, sometimes delicate, with sudden bursts of silence to underscore the unanimity of the effort. Each man is independent yet wholly coordinated with the rest, for they practice constantly and have been playing all their lives. When the gamelan performs, even four- and five-year-olds are allowed to sit next to their brothers and learn how to play the gongs.

There is a fierceness in this percussion music that has its roots in an ancient warrior culture, now softened by centuries of a gentler, more

feminine civilization. The gamelan is used for accompanying all of the village ceremonials. It plays all day when the women take food to the temples to be blessed by the gods, carrying on their heads pyramids of fruits and delicacies piled two or three feet high. (The Balinese are practical people. They take the food home again, after it has all been duly admired and bathed in a sea of music and prayer, so that it can be eaten by the people who produced it.)

The musicians will play all day for a wedding and all night for a dance drama presented at the entrance to one of the temples. There are groups with portable gamelan gongs who take part in the festive cremation ceremonies that are one of the highlights of the Balinese social calendar; they also march in the funeral processions that carry the ashes of the dead down to the beaches in enormous bamboo towers, so that they can be consecrated and carried away by the sea. The towers, carried on the backs of fifteen or twenty young men, are paraded through other villages en route and whirled around in circles every now and then, for the soul of the departed must be prevented from finding its way home, and spinning it around is supposed to make the spirit so dizzy that it will lose its bearings. Meanwhile, the marching sound of the gongs and drums goes on, spreading its invitation throughout the surrounding countryside, so that increasingly large crowds are drawn into the procession.

This is precisely how music was used in the early Mediterranean civilizations, including the Greek and the Roman. Although only a few fragments of classical Greek music have survived, musicologists are certain that Greek songs sounded "Oriental," and that originally the various types of Greek music were as carefully classified as the Indian ragas. "Among us," explains Plato in the *Laws*, "music was divided into various classes and styles; one class of song was that of prayers to the gods, which bore the name of 'hymns'; contrasted with this was another class, best called 'dirges'; 'paeans' formed another; and yet another was the 'dithyramb,' named, I fancy, after Dionysus. 'Nomes' also were so called as being a distinct class of song; and these were further described as 'citharoedic nomes.' So these and other kinds being classified and fixed, it was forbidden to set one kind of words to a different class of tune. . . ." Later, these divisions were disregarded, when, as Plato says, the composers "mixed dirges with hymns and paeans with dithyrambs . . . and blended every kind of music with every other."

Greek life abounded in musical occasions. There were choral songs accompanied by dancing in honor of Apollo and the magical cure dances (like those still practiced by the Sufi dervishes of Persia, in which the patient, placed in the middle of the dance circle, receives the positive vibrations and curative good wishes of those who are dancing around him). There were also the *pyrriche*, or sword dances for young warriors; the *gymnopaidai*, or wrestlinglike dances for unclothed athletes; the *parthenia*, for Spartan virgins; and the choruses and solo songs presented during performances of the great tragedies by Aeschylus, Sophocles, and Euripides and the comedies of Aristophanes (a passage in Aeschylus mentions a chorus of fifty voices).

Besides these ceremonial functions, Greek music also served more

15

humble purposes. The Greeks had work songs for threshing barley, treading grapes, spinning wool, making rope, and drawing water—in fact, music for all the essential peasant tasks. Some of these songs have come down over the centuries almost unscathed, since the need for music and rhythm with such activities never ceases. In many parts of the Mediterranean today, fields cannot be plowed, nor grain threshed, nor almonds gathered except to the accompaniment of work songs whose melodies are at least collateral descendants of those used by the Greeks. In much the same way, the ancient round dances shown on Greek vase paintings survive today, in only slightly modified form, both in Greece itself and in Catalonia, where the Greeks established colonies. Greek and Greco-Roman ceremonial songs were also absorbed into the chants of the Christian Church, and vestiges of them are still sung as part of the Catholic liturgy.

Combining myth and music in equal portions, the ancient Romans created bas-reliefs such as the one shown below, which records an imaginary parade of satyrs playing double flutes led by a maenad carrying a tambourine. The gold figurine at right, thought to be Greek in origin, also depicts a double-flute player.

The music of the early Christian Church, however, had its origins not only in the Greek temples but also in the Jewish synagogues, with their ancient tradition of "song in the house of the Lord, with cymbals, psalteries, and harps" (1 Chron. 25, mentions a total of 228 skilled musicians in the service of Solomon's temple). Portions of the Jewish sacred service—including the "Hallelujah" ("Praise ye the Lord," in Hebrew) and the "Holy, Holy, Holy"—were taken over bodily into the Chris-

tian liturgy; in other cases, traditional synagogue chants were altered to suit Latin texts. Apparently the early Christians also adopted the practices of some of the Hellenistic Jewish sects, such as the antiphonal singing described in the first century A.D. by Philo of Alexandria: "They all stand up together, and ... two choruses are formed ... the one of men and the other of women, and for each chorus there is a leader ... who is the most honorable and most excellent of the band. Then they sing hymns which have been composed in honor of God in many metres and tunes, at one time all singing together, and at another answering one another in a skillful manner."

Many of the early Christian writers mention the importance of singing to the new Church. "The Greeks use Greek, the Romans Latin," writes the third-century theologian Origen. "Everyone prays and sings praises to God as best he can." Saint John Chrysostom, bishop of Constantinople in A.D. 400, wrote that "when God saw that many men were indolent" and too lazy to read the Scriptures, he gave them the music of the Psalms in addition to the words of King David, so that everyone could learn their message by singing joyful hymns: "For nothing so uplifts the mind, giving it wings and freeing it from the earth ... as modulated melody and the divine chant. ..."

The remarks of Saint John Chrysostom on the Psalms suggest that at that time there were no great musical differences between Church chants and the songs of everyday life, for he compares them to the lullabies with which infants are rocked to sleep and to the songs that travelers sing, "driving at noon the yoked animals," to lighten the hardships of the journey. He goes on to describe these everyday songs:

And not only travelers, but also peasants often sing as they tread the grapes in the wine press, gather the vintage, tend the vine, and perform their other tasks. Sailors do likewise, pulling at the oars. Women, too, weaving and parting the tangled threads with the shuttle, often sing a certain melody, sometimes individually and to themselves, sometimes all together in concert. This they do, the women, travelers, peasants and sailors, striving to lighten with a chant the labor endured in working, for the mind suffers hardships and difficulties more easily when it hears songs and chants.

Hebrew, classic Greek, Roman, and Byzantine melodies all helped to form the great body of plain-song liturgy known as Gregorian chant, which, according to tradition, was collected and edited by Pope (afterward Saint) Gregory the Great in the sixth century. It includes more than six hundred compositions for various parts of the Mass, and some three thousand antiphons and responds for the Daily Hours of divine service. In the early Middle Ages, Gregorian chant represented only one of several branches of liturgical tradition within the Western Church. There was the so-called Ambrosian chant of Milan, named for Saint Ambrose; the Visigothic, or Mozarabic, chant of Spain; and the Gallican chant of medieval France. Gradually, however, these others were replaced by the Gregorian liturgy of Rome, with only the Ambrosian chant retaining some of its independence. In the case of the Mozarabic chant, however, the musicologist-monks of the Benedictine monastery of Santo Domingo de Silos, near Burgos, have recently revived the Visigothic rite and restored it to active use for the first time in nearly a thousand years.

Known and sung in all the churches, schools, and monasteries of western Christendom, the Gregorian chant was to have an incalculable influence on subsequent musical developments. It was, indeed, one of the cornerstones on which the whole edifice of European music was to be constructed. Yet the evolution of western music is equally indebted to the profane tradition of folk music and dance—to the "lascivious songs" that Saint John Chrysostom deplored as being the work of "comedians, dancers and harlots," and which, he said, made the mind "softer and weaker." Although these dances and love songs have often drawn the fire of the moralists, they have contributed an incalculable number of new ideas and precedents to the mainstream of music.

Over and over again, the lowliest and most despised beginnings have led to the most magnificent musical developments. The passacaglia form, for example, which Bach used for one of his most resplendent organ works, began life as a popular Spanish dance step whose rhythms were strummed by strolling musicians (and, it is reported, especially by barbers) while passing through the *calles* ("streets")—hence the name. The catchy rhythm of passacaille, as the French called it, soon attracted the attention of serious composers and became the basis of an increasingly complex contrapuntal form employed by some of the foremost baroque masters. A hundred similar examples could be cited. During the nineteenth century, the waltz was at first denounced as the

Church chants, a musical form as ancient as Jerusalem's second Temple, were not collected and systematized until the sixth century A.D. That achievement is traditionally attributed to Pope Gregory; hence the three-voiced chorus featured on the miniature above is said to be singing Gregorian chants. A cappella chanting was ultimately replaced in popularity by more elaborate modes of liturgical accompaniment, including bells, stringed instruments, and bellows organs—all depicted in the thirteenth-century miniature at left, below.

devil's work for placing ladies' waists in the "lewd grasp" of their male partners. Yet Chopin composed some of his most poetic music in "voluptuary" waltz time, and it was to account not only for Richard Strauss's finest operatic moments but also for some of the most powerful episodes in Gustav Mahler's symphonies. Jazz, too, has had a comparable history. In making the long voyage from the brothels of New Orleans to Carnegie Hall, jazz lent its rhythm to a nation and its name to an entire era.

At every stage of history, this glorious pageant of musical invention has fascinated the practitioners of the other arts—the poets and novelists, painters and sculptors. From Geoffrey Chaucer to Thomas Mann, literary men have written vivid pages about musical people. But the most persistent music lovers of all have been the artists who have recorded the visual aspects of the musical life. The results of this love affair can be seen in Egyptian bas-reliefs, Roman mosaics, medieval book illustrations, Italian Renaissance frescoes, French baroque paintings, and countless other works of art in every conceivable medium. Matthias Grünewald paints a concert of angels, and Velásquez the musicians of a Spanish tavern; Veronese paints his self-portrait as a viol player; Rembrandt has the young David playing a harp; Vermeer shows his ladies at the harpsichord; Watteau's gentlemen play lutes; Goya's dandies sing to the guitar; Delacroix portrays Chopin at the piano; Picasso draws a jazz trio as a sheet-music cover for Stravinsky.

Clearly, there is something about music that perpetually appeals to the eye as well as the ear. For one thing, many instruments are very beautiful, since most of them are splendid examples of form following function. But beyond that, the act of making music still retains some of the magic it held for the stone-age dancer playing the mouthbow in the cave of Trois Frères.

Music has become such a piece of everyday magic that one may be hardly conscious of the human and technological miracle that is represented by a phenomenon such as Arthur Rubinstein playing a Liszt sonata or Isaac Stern performing the Beethoven Violin Concerto. As the music-loving Bishop Joseph Hall wrote about lute playing in the seventeenth century:

> Had we lived in some rude and remote part of the world, and should have been told, that it is possible, only by a hollow piece of wood, and the guts of beasts stirred by the fingers of men, to make so sweet and melodious a noise, we should have thought it utterly incredible; yet now that we see and hear it ordinarily done, we make it no wonder.

2

A Royal Road to Song

THE TROUBADOURS CAME RIDING out of the hilltop castles of southern France in the twelfth century, twanging their lutes, fiddling on their viols, and singing magnificent songs that brought several new kinds of civilized pleasure to the courts of Aquitaine and Provence. The times were prosperous and relatively peaceful; trade routes were open, and travel on the highways was no longer a suicidal affair. It was a propitious moment to begin a new movement in the arts of music and poetry.

To be a troubadour was to be both a poet and a composer (the word comes from the verb *trobar*, to compose), for no one ever considered one without the other. As the troubadour Folquet de Marseilles says in one of his songs, "A verse without music is a mill without water." Their language was that form of medieval Romance spoken throughout southern France and now known as Provençal. In this very supple and expressive idiom they wrote songs about things that were too personal, too passionate to be phrased in monkish Latin—and thus they created the first lyric poetry in any modern European language. They sang about love, sex, and politics, about the physical and mental pleasures to be derived from courtship in accordance with the rules of the *ars amatoria*, the "arts of love." A "pleasant fever" is what Guillaume de Cabestaing calls it in his song *Li dous cossire*:

> That pleasant fever
> That love doth often bring
> Lady, doth ever
> Attune the songs I sing
> Where I endeavor
> To catch again your chaste
> Sweet body's savor
> I crave but may not taste.

The troubadours' paeans to chivalric love were a principal source of diversion in medieval Europe. As the revelers of the fanciful manuscript illumination opposite attest, the age was not one of mere idealized passion.

To the troubadours, love was an experience to be cultivated, prolonged, intensified, and cherished as one of the great gifts of civilization. It was not, as has sometimes been claimed, that the woman's inaccessibility had to be taken for granted. On the contrary, most of the troubadour songs contain declarations of intent couched in much stronger terms than the Beatles' "I Want to Hold Your Hand." The great troubadour Arnaud Daniel, for example, looks forward to being with his lady so that he can feel "the great joy of having her, amid kisses and laughter, disclose her fair body that I may gaze at it beneath the lamplight." Bernart de Ventadour expresses the hope that his love will have the courage "to have me come one night there where she undresses and make me a necklace of her arms." Duke William of Aquitaine, who is considered the first of the troubadours, describes himself as an "infallible master," not on account of his songs but because "there is no woman who, after a night with me, will not want me back the next day." And Bertrand de Born, Viscount of Hautefort, describes his mistress—and the twelfth century's feminine ideal—as a lady "delicate and fair, charming, gay and young; her hair is blond

Ferrara, the ducal seat of the Este family, was one of Renaissance Italy's notable musical milieus. The Este palace itself was decorated with elaborate allegorical frescoes, each devoted to a given month and each built upon a musical theme. April's delights are arrayed below.

with a ruby tint, her body white as hawthorne, with soft arms and firm breasts and a rabbit's suppleness in her back."

Besides singing of love, the troubadours also served as the news commentators of their day. Since the printing press was not to be invented for another three hundred years, there was virtually no other way of disseminating the latest news. In the songs known as sirventés, the troubadours discussed current affairs, politics, personalities, the latest fashions and scandals, and the "joyful season" of war, when the knights had a chance to test their training and equipment on the field of battle. Bertrand de Born became famous for writing warmongering songs that stirred up the barons and provoked kings into going to war

with one another. To Bertrand, war was the continuation of poetry by other means:

> I love to see the press of shields
> With their hues of red and blue
> Of ensigns and of banners
> manycolored in the wind,
> and the sight of tents and rich pavilions pitched,
> lances shattered, shields pierced, shining
> helmets split, and blows exchanged in battle.

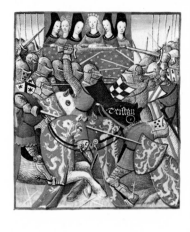

In theory, troubadours were supposed to be belted knights, but in practice they came from all walks of life. Like the pop composers of the twentieth century, many of them became rich and famous by taking their songs from court to court, where the great princes might reward them with horses, armor, or feudal privileges. The ideal patron of the arts was someone like Blacatz, Lord of Aups in the early thirteenth century, who also enjoyed a considerable reputation as a troubadour: "And he delighted in ladies, and love, and war, and spending, and feasting, and tumult, and music, and song, and play, and all such things as give a good man worth and fame. Never was there a man who loved better to take than he to give."

Like composers of a later day, some of the troubadours hired professional singers and entertainers (*jongleurs*) to perform their works,

Originally written to celebrate such wholly secular occasions as the jousting tournament seen above, the songs of the troubadours were subsequently adapted for exclusively religious purposes. The renowned Cantigas de Santa Maria, *which were produced under the supervision of Alfonso the Wise of Castile, recorded those songs for posterity. And as the illustrations at left, below, and at right indicate, the* Cantigas *also provided graphic evidence of the extraordinary range of instruments available to thirteenth-century musicians.*

since their own voices were often unequal to the task of displaying their songs to advantage. What their music was like no one knows for certain. It has been preserved in a handful of early manuscripts that indicate only the melodic outline of each song, but not the rhythm or accompaniment. Some of the miniatures of this period, however, show troubadours and minstrels accompanying themselves on lutes, viols, or early forerunners of the guitar. In any case, a well-equipped thirteenth-century castle was apt to have a music room full of instruments with which to accompany songs, dances, and ceremonials.

The richest source of pictures of medieval musicmaking is one of the manuscripts of the *Cantigas de Santa Maria*, produced at the court of Alfonso the Wise, a thirteenth-century ruler of Castile. He was one of the last to cultivate troubadour poetry, and one of the first to adapt it to religious purposes, calling himself a "troubadour of Saint Mary." The miniatures of the *Cantigas* show the whole incredible range of instruments available to a great court in the Middle Ages. There are musicians playing metal trumpets and ivory horns, lutes of all sizes, vielles plucked and bowed, gitterns, rebecs, psalteries, harps, mandolas, organistra (hurdy-gurdies), chime bells, cymbals, castanets, tabors and tabor-pipes, bagpipes, recorders, flutes, shawms and double-shawms (two primitive clarinets with their mouthpieces bound together), and a great many others whose precise names are no longer known. These instruments are the ancestors of those in the modern symphony orchestra. Their function, however, was not to play together to produce a pattern of harmonies (that idea had not yet occurred to anyone) but to play singly, in pairs, or in small groups to punctuate the rhythm of a dance or to accompany the solo voice in unison and at the octave, supporting the melody and supplying a sort of drone for it.

Most of these instruments had originated in the Near East and had

come to Europe via the Moorish kingdoms of southern Spain, which had been under Arab domination since the eighth century. In the course of their conquests, the Arabs had taken over the ancient civilization of Persia and had imported it, in turn, into their magnificent courts at Córdoba, Seville, and Granada. Their culture was so obviously superior to the rude life-style of the Christian kingdoms in northern Spain that, despite the incessant warfare between them, the Christian kings soon felt obliged to match the Moslem emirs in music, literature, and the visual arts. Indeed, the illustrations of Alfonso's songs in honor of Saint Mary show that Moorish minstrels were among the musicians of his court; perhaps as many as fifty percent of his musicians were of Moorish origin. Spain thus served as the gateway through which much of Persian and Arabic culture entered Europe—an influence that included every sort of eastern instrument from kettledrums to lutes.

But the musical culture of Europe was destined to follow its own unique path of development, which was to produce an art that had very little in common with musical styles from other parts of the world. It was a royal road that led from the monody of Gregorian chant to the complex polyphony of the Renaissance masters; from the troubadours with their lute accompaniments to the great choral and instrumental aggregations of the baroque era.

In Europe, far more than anywhere else, music became a matter of social organization and applied technology. For the consecration of Salzburg Cathedral in 1628, for example, the Italian composer Orazio Benevoli wrote a festival Mass that almost rivals the architecture of the cathedral in the intricacies of its colossal plan. It has two eight-part

At the same time that Gothic cathedrals such as Chartres (left)
were rising across Western Europe, polyphony was in the
process of supplanting monody.
The multivoiced chorus was a
regular feature of church services, and scenes such as the one
depicted at right by Giovannino
di Grassi were commonplace.
During Grassi's day musical notation was all but nonexistent,
and choristers "read" music from
specially annotated scrolls. By
the end of the fifteenth century,
however, hymnals had largely replaced such scrolls—as the detail
below, from a contemporary
treatise on music, indicates.

choruses, each with two solo quartets and an organ, and each accompanied by an instrumental ensemble. One of these orchestras consists of a
six-part body of violins and violas, an eight-part wind band of oboes,
flutes, and trumpets, and another section of two trumpets and three
trombones. The second chorus is accompanied by comparable forces,
among them eight trumpeters and four kettledrummers. The immense
group that provides the thorough bass includes cellos, contrabasses, bassoons, harpsichords, harps, and lutes. The individual parts of the Mass
total fifty-three, necessitating a score page nearly three feet long. It is
as though Bernini's gigantic colonnades in St. Peter's Square had been
transformed into music.

The key to such a vast sound-producing enterprise is the score,
which provides the only practical means by which the work can be
planned and executed. Other cultures have sometimes brought together
great numbers of voices and instruments for temple rituals, but they
have had to do without the master plan that directs the activities of the
symphony orchestra. It is the "script culture" of the West that deter-
mines the essential distinction between a Balinese gamelan orchestra and

the Vienna Philharmonic. The fifty-three separate melodic strands of Benevoli's Mass had to be charted visually before they could be coordinated aurally. For that matter, even the relative simplicity of a four-voiced Bach fugue could never have come about without the prior existence of a system of notation, unique to the West, that enables a composer to express his musical ideas on paper, in a graph that can be read and executed by any well-trained musician.

This system is responsible not only for some of the stylistic differences between the Eastern and Western approaches to music; it also accounts for a vital philosophical distinction. An Indian sitar player must be adept at choosing the raga for the particular moment of his performance, and his choice will reflect the season of the year, the time of day, and his own mood as well as that of his listeners. He improvises, of course, and he perceives music as a transitory phenomenon that lives

and dies with each performance. To a composer in the Western tradition, his score is a kind of permanent monument that will outlive him and which exists forever in an ideal, Platonic dimension. Any particular performance can only be an approximation of the theoretical perfection of the score. As a result, many composers have written at least some of their music, as did Beethoven or Anton von Webern, not for their own time but "for a future age." This idea would never occur to an Oriental musician, whose medium is the here and now.

The long road from the troubadours to the baroque era is a thoroughly international one, leading through every country of Western Europe and touching all levels of culture. Around the year 1200, to coincide with the beginnings of great cathedrals like those of Notre Dame in Paris, and at Rheims and Rouen, the first two- and three-voiced church music began to make its appearance. This school of primitive polyphony was known as organum, and its earliest representatives were Magister Leoninus of Notre Dame and his successor, the choirmaster Perotinus. A century later, at about the time Dante was at work on *La Vita Nuova* and the *Divine Comedy*, the rigid discipline of this dissonant style (the *ars antiqua*) gave way to the freedom of the *ars nova*, brilliantly propounded by the French poet and musician Guillaume de Machaut, who discovered many new ways of setting note against note and point *contra* point.

The 1380's—the age of Geoffrey Chaucer's *Canterbury Tales* in England—saw the first flowering of the Italian madrigal in Florence (the word comes from *matricale*, a pastoral in the mother tongue as opposed to Latin) and the beginnings of the Meistersinger movement in Germany (five hundred years later, Richard Wagner was to make this the subject of his only comic opera). In 1415, when Henry V of England defeated the French at Agincourt, the English school of composers, headed by John Dunstable and Lionel Power, was at work on the

The Renaissance produced scores of great composers, among them (from left to right) Orlando di Lasso, known throughout Europe as "the prince of musicians"; Giovanni Pierluigi da Palestrina, renowned composer of religious music; Giovanni Battista Lully, royal composer to Louis XIV; François Couperin, noted scion of a famous musical family; Jean Philippe Rameau, supreme musical theorist; and Claudio Monteverdi, progenitor of opera.

Overleaf: The lute and the virginal are said to have been the most popular instruments in sixteenth-century Venice, where music lessons such as this one were a part of every gentlewoman's upbringing.

first musically unified choral Masses, together with motets (sacred compositions for several voices) and French chansons. A generation later, as the Flemish brothers Hubert and Jan van Eyck were producing their famous musical altar painting for the cathedral at Ghent, a new school of counterpoint arose in Burgundy under Guillaume Dufay, a technical innovator who wrote sacred and secular music in a great variety of styles.

Around 1500, while Leonardo da Vinci was painting the *Mona Lisa* and Michelangelo the Sistine ceiling, the great Flemish composer Josquin Des Prés was active in Italy. (His first book of Masses was published in Venice in 1503.) Josquin has been called the Raphael of music, for both he and the great Italian painter prepared the way for the baroque age. Before Josquin, music was primarily concerned with structural principles, but it was his example that shifted the emphasis to emotional expressiveness and "the passions of the soul in music."

In Germany, around 1530, the Protestant Reformation brought the

Lutheran chorale—and with it, a new folk spirit—into church music. Italy, at about the same time, witnessed the second golden age of the madrigal; literally thousands of such songs were produced by native Italian and visiting Flemish composers. Among the Netherlanders in Italy were Adrien Willaert (who established a school in Venice), Cipriano de Rore, Philippe de Monte, and Roland de Lassus, alias Orlando di Lasso, known throughout Europe as "the prince of musicians." From Italy, Lassus went on to Munich to become music director to the Duke of Bavaria. He wrote two thousand works in Latin, Italian, German, and French, received a patent of nobility from the Emperor Maximilian, and was decorated with the Order of the Golden Spur by Pope Gregory XIII.

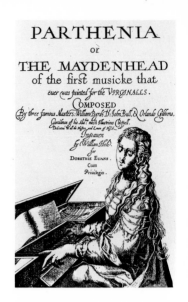

Another master of the madrigal was Giovanni Pierluigi da Palestrina, foremost of the composers who served at the papal court in Rome. His

secular achievements are overshadowed by his work in perfecting the great a cappella Masses with their smoothly flowing counterpoint and harmonic buoyancy. In Spain, meanwhile, Luis Milan, Alonso de Mudarra, and several other virtuosos on the guitarlike vihuela created the first truly instrumental idiom that was not simply a translation from the vocal style. During the age of Cervantes, in the latter part of the sixteenth century, the greatest of Spanish composers was Tomás Luis de Victoria, who succeeded Palestrina in the pontifical chapel. In England, Shakespeare's musical contemporaries were William Byrd, Thomas Morley, and John Bull, all of them devoted to writing pavanes and other dances for the virginals (an early form of harpsichord) as well as the more conventional vocal forms.

Instrumental music had been steadily gaining in importance during this period and began coming into its own about 1600. Freed from the necessity of accompanying words, music now moved to dance rhythms rather than speech rhythms; the sound of viol consorts and other chamber ensembles was heard in the land. Claudio Monteverdi, the first of the great Italian operatic composers (and the last madrigalist) was also the first to explore the tone-color resources of the orchestra. He revolutionized performing techniques with such devices as the tremolo and pizzicato in the strings.

The golden age of baroque instrumental music really begins with

The virginal at lower left once belonged to Elizabeth I, and the instrument's name may well derive from its association with the Virgin Queen. In any case, the virginal enjoyed immense popularity in sixteenth-century England—a fact reflected in the publication of music books (left) especially for that instrument. Music was also a vital dimension of French court life, as the contemporary portrait below of Louis XIV surrounded by court musicians indicates. The Sun King himself was reputed to be a skilled dancer and guitarist.

Overleaf: Venice became the pleasure capital of eighteenth-century Europe, and scores of international visitors crowded the lagoon city to hear concerts such as the one depicted in Francesco Guardi's painting.

orchestral combinations such as the one Monteverdi employed in the first performance of his opera *Orfeo,* presented to celebrate the wedding of the Duke of Mantua in 1607. It consisted of two harpsichords, two contrabasses, twelve members of the violin family, a double harp, two archlutes, two organs with wooden pipes, a small portable organ, three viola da gambas, four trombones, two cornets, a small flute, a clarino trumpet, three muted trumpets, and further assistance from harp, flute, and zither. With these Monteverdi dramatized his characters and situations: a shepherd is accompanied by the high flute and a small violin; the underworld is suggested by brasses and organ music; Orpheus' entreaties are underscored by the strains of a harp; the spirits of the netherworld whisper in Flemish counterpoint.

Thirty years later, while the young Rembrandt was at work in Amsterdam and the aged Galileo went before the Inquisition in Rome for advocating the idea that the earth revolves around the sun, the German composer Heinrich Schütz created a brilliant series of dramatic oratorios on biblical themes—although the development of his gifts was hampered by the disastrous effects of the Thirty Years' War. In France, the son of a poor Italian miller, Giovanni Battista Lully, became viceroy of music at the court of that redoubtable monarch Louis XIV, for whom Lully produced a steady stream of operas, ballets, and ceremonial suites.

Louis himself was a skilled guitarist and dancer (for twenty-two years he took daily lessons from his dancing master, Pierre Beauchamps), and he took an active interest in the musical affairs of Versailles. In 1693 he personally presided over a competition to select a new organist for the royal chapel. A young and unknown organist was chosen when Louis commented to the other judges, "I shall be glad to know your opinion; in my own judgment, it is this young man I never heard of before who played best and seems to me the most worthy." It was François Couperin, afterwards known as "Le Grand" to distinguish him from the rest of the very numerous clan of musical Couperins. Louis soon knighted him for his services to the Crown in creating a brilliant and distinctive style of French keyboard music—a task that was to be completed after his death by another ingenious clavecinist, Jean Philippe Rameau.

In Restoration England, meanwhile, musical life under Charles II and his immediate successors was dominated by Henry Purcell, who became organist of Westminster Abbey at the age of twenty. His church and ceremonial music was so expressive that some of his listen-

The word concerto *is Italian in origin, reflecting the fact that musical history's most prolific writer of concertos was a Venetian named Antonio Vivaldi (above). The intimate musical performance at left was captured by Venetian painter Pietro Longhi.*

ers were moved to wonder whether "they ever heard any thing so rapturously fine and solemn and Heavenly in Operation." But Purcell also composed the catchiest theater music of the time and some of the most ribald songs ever written.

In Italy, where the great violin makers were concentrated, chiefly in Verona, it was the violin virtuosos who were perfecting new forms and styles of instrumental music. (The terms *concerto, sinfonia,* and *sonata* all arose out of Italian usage, although their precise "classical" meanings were not to be defined until the latter part of the eighteenth century.) Among the violinist-composers were Giovanni Vitali, Giuseppe Torelli, Arcangelo Corelli, and Giuseppe Tartini. But the one destined to become best known was Antonio Vivaldi, the musical director of the orphanage-conservatory of the Ospedale della Pietà in Venice. It was here, in the early eighteenth century, with an all-girl orchestra, that Vivaldi wrote most of his five hundred concertos, the majority of them scored for violin or various combinations of strings. The girls gave a public concert every Sunday, and their programs were constantly changed; hence the need for such vast amounts of new music. The French traveler Charles de Brosses described the ensemble:

> They sing like angels and play the violin, the flute, the organ, the cello, and the bassoon; in short, there is no instrument, however unwieldy, that can frighten them. They are cloistered like nuns. It is they alone who perform, and about forty girls take part in each concert. I vow to you that there is nothing so diverting as the sight of a young and pretty nun in a white habit, with a bunch of pomegranate blossoms over her ear, conducting the orchestra and beating time with all the grace and precision imaginable.

Certainly the art of music had come a long way in the five hundred years since the troubadours; only the underlying motives for music-making had remained unchanged. Above all it was still a feast for aural sensualists. As Samuel Pepys confided to his diary, "music is all the pleasure that I live for in the world, and the greatest I can ever expect in the best of my life." It would have been difficult to find a cultivated man in the baroque era who would have disagreed with him. The fact that music now possessed an enormous arsenal of ways and means, of forms and effects, only increased the power that it exerted on men's minds. Perhaps it never stood higher in prestige than at that moment in history, when it had acquired an almost magical ability to enthrall the sedulous ear with gorgeous instrumental colors and magnificent harmonies. When Pepys went to see a musical performance in 1688, he observed afterward that the sounds had taken "real command" of his soul, and that he had remained in transports of delight the whole night through. "That which did please me beyond anything in the whole world was the wind-musique when the angel comes down, which is so sweet that it ravished me, and indeed, in a word, did wrap up my soul so that it made me really sick, just as I have formerly been when in love with my wife."

41

3

The Splendor of Bach

HE WAS A STRANGER in the town and struck up an acquaintance with the local organist, explaining that he belonged to the same profession. Since the local organist was known to be a musician of considerable ability, and his church was one of those which contained two organs, it seemed only natural that the stranger should suggest a trial of skills. They would improvise on the two organs in question-and-answer fashion, playing the game known as "leading each other astray" while extemporizing fantasias in various styles of counterpoint.

For a time the contest sounded like an equal match. The two organists took turns, each picking up where the other had left off, tossing musical challenges back and forth. It seemed at first as if the four hands and four feet were directed by a single head. But gradually the visiting virtuoso began to employ the more recondite arts of counter-. point and modulation. He stretched out his fugue subjects by augmentation and compressed them by diminution; he turned them upside down and right side up again; he made them suddenly overlap or combined them with seemingly unrelated themes in a complex web of sound, as he discovered ingenious ways of slipping into unexpected keys. The local organist observed what the other man was doing and tried to imitate him, but soon he could no longer keep up the pace. Whenever he faltered, the visitor would help him recover his equilibrium. Then he would lead the way into new mazes of harmony from which the host, in the end, could no longer extricate himself. At last he jumped up from the keyboard and ran over to the stranger, conceding himself beaten but entreating his guest to go on playing as long as he might, for "You must be either Sebastian Bach or an angel from heaven!"

Baroque organs were not designed to produce the diminishing and swelling tones familiar to us, but rather were known for clarity, lightness, and contrast. The organ at left is in Bologna's Church of San Michele.

It was indeed the great Johann Sebastian Bach, with whom the local organist would not have attempted to match wits had he known his identity. This is one of the stories told about Bach by the theorist F. W. Marpurg, who knew the composer personally and may have heard the tale from Bach himself. To engage in a keyboard duel with Bach was something few virtuosos of the day were rash enough to try— hence the need for incognito and subterfuge in looking for a sparring partner. Some of his rivals had been known to leave town in a hurry rather than face the prospect of a public confrontation with him. A great deal of prestige was at stake in these contests, for to excel in the art of improvisation was a matter of particular pride among baroque

Johann Sebastian Bach (left, in Elias G. Haussmann's 1741 portrait) was born in the quiet Thuringian town of Eisenach, shown opposite, below. He heard himself lauded as a virtuoso organist rather than finding acclaim during his lifetime for the hundreds of works he produced; a page from one of his violin sonatas is at right.

organists; they considered it the highest test of their musicianship. And Bach was acknowledged to be the master of them all.

His fame as "the greatest organ and harpsichord player we have ever seen" brought him a great many invitations to serve as official examiner of the splendid organs that were being built throughout northern Germany in the early eighteenth century. On the social calendar of a sleepy Saxon town like Naumburg or Halle it was always a major event when Bach arrived to inaugurate a new organ. In those pious days virtually everyone went to church, and an organ was often their only source of Sunday entertainment, besides being as advanced and impressive a piece of precision machinery as anyone was ever apt to see.

In putting the instrument through its paces, Bach would give a breathtaking demonstration of fingerwork on the manuals and footwork on the pedals. His earliest biographer, J. N. Forkel, describes how, after seating himself at the organ, Bach would

> . . . choose some one theme and develop it in the various forms of organ composition, but in such a way that his material was always based on

this same subject, even when he played uninterruptedly for two hours or more. First he would use this theme for a prelude and fugue with full organ. Then he would display his art of using the stops, for a trio, quartet, etc., still on the same subject. Afterward followed a chorale, whose melody was again playfully surrounded ... with a fugue on the full organ, in which either another treatment of only the first subject might predominate, or, depending on its nature, one or two other subjects might be mixed with it.

When Bach played like this on a visit to Hamburg in 1720, improvising for half an hour on the chorale *By the Waters of Babylon*, the ninety-seven-year-old organ master Adam Reinken said to him, "I thought this art was dead, but I see that it still lives, in you."

It was true, however, that Bach was the representative of a dying art. He had the misfortune to be born thirty years too late, for counterpoint was going out of style, and his contemporaries were far more fascinated with the lighter, less polyphonic music of the Italian opera. His music was considered old fashioned, if not actually obsolete. "This great man would be the admiration of whole nations if he had more charm," wrote a Hamburg critic in 1737, "and if he did not diminish the natural quality of his pieces with his turgid and confused style, darkening their beauty with all-too-excessive art." Although some of his admirers rushed to his defense, none of them would have denied that he was the last of a vanishing race of great contrapuntalists. And no one at the time could have foreseen that within a hundred years every serious composer would come to regard Bach as the "founding father" of music and "the demigod of our art," as Schumann called him.

Tastes change, of course, and many earlier composers have since joined the pantheon, but the musical world still refers to them as the "pre-Bach" composers, in tacit recognition of his unique position at the Great Divide of music history. After more than two centuries, moreover, Bach is still pre-eminently the composer from whom the others like to borrow their ideas. Since the first Bach revival of the 1800's, he has been an inexhaustible source of inspiration to everyone from Bee-

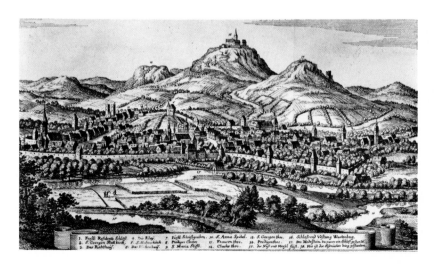

thoven and Brahms to Ferruccio Busoni, Igor Stravinsky, Dave Brubeck, and the Beatles. The Swingle Singers perform him in skat-singing style, Jacques Loussier with a jazz combo, Walter Carlos with an electronic sound synthesizer. Clearly, everyone indulges in Bach cribbing not on account of his historical importance but because his music is tremendously alive and full of harmonic surprises, or what Stravinsky called "the wonderful jolts, the sudden modulations, the unexpected harmonic changes, the deceptive cadences, that are the joy of every Bach cantata." Paradoxically, Bach the great contrapuntalist is also Bach the great harmonist. When modern jazzmen and pop groups steal from him, what they covet most are his harmonic progressions, which contain some of the most excruciatingly beautiful dissonances in the whole literature of music.

But the harmonies that now fascinate jazzmen and connoisseurs often baffled the solid Saxon burghers who constituted the bulk of his audience. In Arnstadt, for example, where Bach worked for four years as organist—it was his first job—the town consistory once lodged an official complaint against him for having "made many curious *variationes* in the chorale and mixed many strange tones into it, so that the congregation has become confused thereby." For that matter, most of the source documents for a biography of Bach are in the form of complaints of one kind or another—about the dissonances in his conduct as well as in his music. They are to be found in obscure town records or court archives, and the picture that emerges from between the lines is that of an energetic, headstrong, and rather irritable personality not even remotely resembling an angel from heaven.

In 1705 there is mention of a street brawl in which the twenty-year-old Bach was attacked by five bullies led by a member of his church choir whom he had provoked with the dreadful epithet *Zippel-faggotist*—"nanny-goat bassoonist." Another complaint was lodged against the young organist for having made his chorale prelude too long, "but after his attention had been drawn to it by the Superintendent, he had at once fallen into the other extreme and made it too short." Then there is another, more intriguing, charge that he allowed a "stranger maiden" to visit the organ loft and make music there. That would have been his second cousin Maria Barbara Bach, an organist's daughter (all the Bachs, for seven generations, were church or town musicians in Thuringia, as was Sebastian's own father, Johann Ambrosius). She was soon to become the first of two wives who bore him the now-legendary total of twenty children. What makes this a somewhat misleading statistic is that ten of his children died in infancy; of those that remained, five became well-known professional musicians.

In 1708, the year after his marriage, Bach entered the service of the Duke of Weimar, whose musical establishment included "sixteen well-disciplined musicians clad in Hungarian *haiduk* uniforms." After a decade in Weimar the court archives record a rather more serious complaint than usual: "On November 6, the former concertmeister and organist Bach was confined to the county judge's place of detention on account of the stiff-necked obstinacy with which he expressed his insistence on being dismissed, and finally on December 2 was freed

The harpsichord above was Bach's, built for him by Gottfried Silberman, who also experimented with the piano, a new instrument that never satisfied Bach—although it gradually eclipsed the harpsichord in popularity. Another popular instrument was the flute, being played at right in a portrait by Johann Hapetzky.

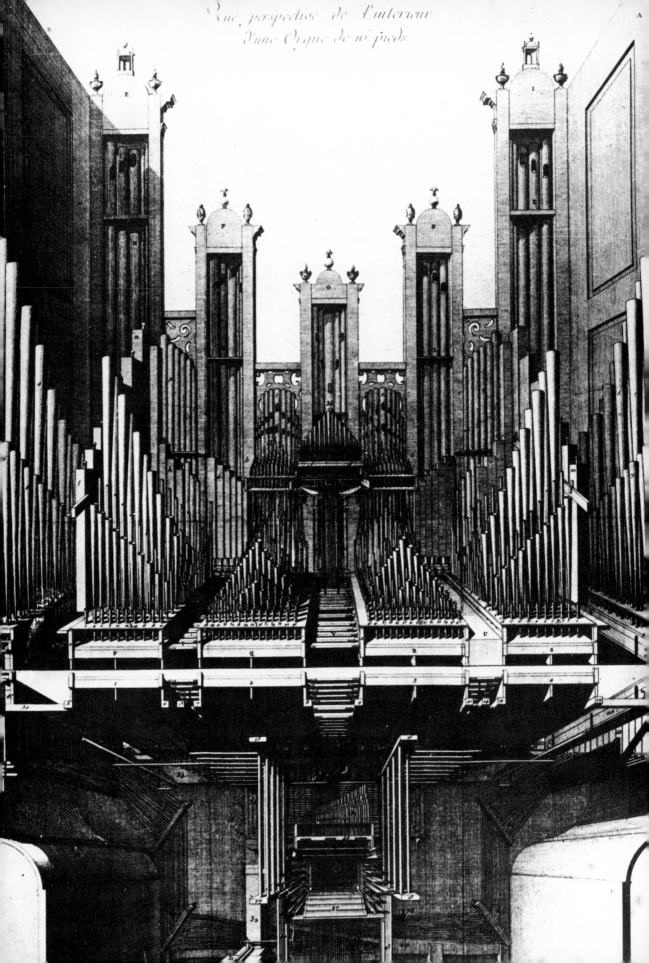

Vue perspective de l'interieur
d'une Orgue de 16 pieds.

The Lutheran Church of Saint Thomas in Leipzig opened onto a busy street (above) from which parishoners stepped every Sunday into a vaulted interior (top). After hearing a Scripture reading, they listened to a scant choir and a dozen instrumentalists take part in one of Bach's specially composed cantatas elaborating on the Scripture; Bach himself led the music at an organ similar to the one shown opposite.

Overleaf: Angels holding a score gaze impassively from this fresco painted in the Cathedral of Udine, Italy, by a younger contemporary of Bach's, Giovanni Battista Tiepolo.

from arrest with notice of his unfavorable discharge." It was a forcible reminder, if he needed it, that the feudal system was still in effect.

A new post was waiting for him at the diminutive court of Anhalt-Cöthen, sixty miles away. As musical director to the young prince of Anhalt-Cöthen, he had charge of a seventeen-man orchestra largely staffed with men of solo caliber. It was for them that he wrote his great instrumental suites as well as the six *Brandenburg Concertos*, named for the Prussian prince to whom they were dedicated but modeled on the Italian concerto grosso form. Bach was acquainted with a great deal of Italian music, and the lyric, expressive melodies of composers like Vivaldi and Corelli had made a deep impression on him. Ultimately he was to bring north and south into a perfect equilibrium, spinning out a tracery of independent melodies over a solid harmonic bass. The result is a combination of logic and fantasy: the German fugue married to the Italian aria. His orchestrations were always designed to take maximum advantages of any virtuoso players who happened to be at his disposal. The second *Brandenburg Concerto*, for example, is written for a solo group of flute, oboe, violin, and trumpet who engage in animated conversation among themselves and with the main body of strings.

At Anhalt-Cöthen, Bach also composed a systematic series of keyboard studies ranging from the simplest *Two-Part Inventions* for the education of his children to the formidable bravura pieces in Book I of *The Well-Tempered Clavier*. His purpose in writing the *Clavier* was to demonstrate the advantages of his preferred method of tuning ("tempering") a harpsichord and to explore the musical characteristics of the twenty-four major and minor keys by writing a prelude and fugue appropriate to each of them. But it was destined to become the bible of keyboard playing. Even Chopin, whose style is so very different from Bach's, considered it "the highest and best school" of pianism and always warmed up for his concerts by playing the *Clavier*.

In 1723 Bach resigned his post at Anhalt-Cöthen to become cantor (music director) at St. Thomas' School in Leipzig. Here the record of complaints, both by and against him, begins again and mounts to a dissonant crescendo. He seems to have spent much of his time in a long series of squabbles with pettifogging church and town authorities to whom he was to become known as the "incorrigible" cantor. His principal duties were to direct the music for four Leipzig churches as well as the training of choirboys at St. Thomas'. But the post was not as lucrative as he had been led to expect, and Leipzig was very expensive. Besides, as he wrote to a friend, the authorities were so unmusical and uncooperative "that I must live amid almost constant vexation, envy and persecution. ... My situation here is worth about seven hundred taler, and when there are more bodies than *ordinairement*, the funeral fees rise in proportion. But when a healthy wind blows, they fall accordingly; last year, for example, I lost over one hundred taler that would ordinarily have come in from corpse fees (*Leichen accidentia*)."

Bach tried to organize an efficient musical establishment but was frustrated by the town council's refusal to appropriate sufficient funds for it. In one of his reports to the authorities he drew up a list of those choristers who were "usable," those who needed further training, and

those, alas, who were not musicians at all. The final balance sheet: seventeen usable, twenty potentials, seventeen unfit. Ideally, Bach said, he would like a chorus of sixteen trained singers for each church and an orchestra of at least eighteen men—eleven strings, two oboes, bassoon, three trumpets, and tympani—to accompany the cantata of the week, which was performed in only one church at a time. The orchestra he actually had to work with, however, was a terrible comedown from Anhalt-Cöthen: "four town pipers, three professional fiddlers and one apprentice." That meant he had to recruit volunteers from the University of Leipzig, a task made more difficult by the council's refusal to pay them the usual fees. Yet these were the forces for whom he wrote the great majority of his choral masterpieces—266 of his 295 church cantatas (only two-thirds of which have been preserved), the Magnificat in D Minor, the Mass in B Minor, and the two dramatic settings of the gospel narrative for Good Friday, *The Passion According to St. Matthew* and *The Passion According to St. John*.

Although this adds up to a vast amount of music, much of which had to be written on a clockwork schedule, Bach never treated any of these as routine assignments. Every cantata shows evidence of having been lovingly worked over, especially in the cryptic musical puns and contrapuntal allusions that were obviously meant only for the eyes and ears of the initiated. The cantata texts are full of images that are pictorially illustrated in the accompaniment: the splashing of waves, the bounding of stags on the hills, the shedding of tears in chromatic pain. In one case, where the text mentions joy, the singers burst into a twenty-five-note "paroxysm" of laughter; in another, based on the parable of the seven wise and the seven foolish virgins and their responses to the coming of the bridegroom, the orchestra maintains the steady beat of a wedding march while the chorus sings a Lutheran chorale punctuated with shouts of "Wake Up! Wake Up!"

Toward the end of his life, Bach evidently felt the need to preserve and systematize his matchless knowledge of polyphony, for the works that he composed, engraved, and privately printed during the 1740's constitute a giant compendium of the contrapuntal arts and crafts. In the *Goldberg Variations*, ostensibly written so that his pupil J. G. Goldberg could entertain Count Kayserling on sleepless nights, a simple household tune is turned into a set of thirty ingenious variations, of which every third one is based on a different sort of canon. Another demonstration of polyphonic alchemy is the dazzling set of organ variations on the Christmas chorale *Vom Himmel Hoch*, which Bach presented to a Leipzig musical society in lieu of an inaugural address. These variations culminate in a cascade of canons like a shower of stars. His visit to Frederick the Great of Prussia in 1747 produced *The Musical Offering*, in which he explored the fugal possibilities of the "right Royal theme" that Frederick had suggested to him as a subject for improvisation. Having shown what he could do with an amateur's theme, he then proceeded to subject one of his own to the same process. In *The Art of the Fugue* the basic theme is transformed into a series of increasingly complex fugues and canons to illustrate some of the limitless ways in which a fugue subject could be combined, com-

The baroque was an age of skilled performers—from soloists like the violinist shown sitting comfortably before his score (above) to ensemble musicians (right) who could probably play one another's instruments with equally cheerful countenances. Among these virtuosos, Domenico Scarlatti (above, right, in a retrospective portrait) was often ranked as the best harpsichordist of his day.

pressed, expanded, turned upside down, and run off backward.

Most of *The Art of the Fugue* was engraved under Bach's supervision, but blindness prevented him from finishing the great triple (or perhaps quadruple) fugue that introduces his four-note signature theme, B-A-C-H (a musical spelling that works only in German notation; in English practice, the notes are known as B-flat-A-C-B). Thus the last and most difficult contrapunctus of all breaks off in mid-flight at the two hundred and thirty-ninth measure. When Bach, having suffered a stroke, felt that death was near, he dictated to his son-in-law a chorale prelude on the hymn *Wenn wir in höchsten Nöten seyn* ("When We Are in Greatest Need"), but as a superscription he chose the first line of another stanza: *Vor deinen Thron tret' ich hiemit* ("With this I step before Thy Throne"). His death, at sixty-five, in 1750 "was uncommonly mourned by all true connoisseurs of music," as a Leipzig newspaper reported. But the town council merely used the occasion to complete the record by registering one last complaint about their incorrigible cantor.

Bach and his two great contemporaries George Frederick Handel and Domenico Scarlatti all happened to be born in the same year, 1685, but each represents a different facet of baroque music—let the astrologers make of that what they may. Bach, born under the sign of Aries (March 21), personifies the splendor of German Protestant church

music; he is the genius on the organ bench, adept at manipulating that technological miracle, the baroque organ, and its necessary adjunct, the church choir. Handel, born on February 23 (Pisces), embodied the theatrical spirit of the high baroque, a time when "all that impresses mankind is theatrical," as the critic Johann Mattheson wrote in 1728, "The whole world is a giant theater." As for the Scorpio, Scarlatti (born on October 26), he epitomizes the court composer, and his music is that of the Mediterranean palaces, with their baroque flourishes and arabesques.

Handel and Scarlatti became acquainted in Rome during the former's Italian journey (neither of them ever met Bach). The meeting probably took place in 1709 at the palace of Cardinal Ottoboni, who brought the two composers together for the inevitable trial of skill. "The issue of the trial on the harpsichord has been differently reported," writes Handel's first biographer, John Mainwaring. "It has been said that some gave the preference to Scarlatti. However, when it came to the organ there was not the least pretence for doubting to which of them it belonged. Scarlatti himself declared the superiority of his antagonist." Mainwaring reports that Handel often spoke of Scarlatti with great admiration, "for besides his great talents as an artist, he had the sweetest temper, and the genteelest behavior." Scarlatti, meanwhile, if complimented on his playing, "would mention Handel, and cross himself in token of veneration." Scarlatti was known for his "elegance and delicacy of expression," although he possessed a technique so formidable that one witness said it sounded as though "ten hundred

The making of music depended upon patrons, from the hundreds of aristocrats who treated their friends to concerts (left, below) to George elector of Hanover and later king of England who sponsored the compositions of George Frederick Handel, above. The reigning duke had persuaded Handel's worried father that it was perfectly acceptable to let the boy study music.

Overleaf: The elegant charm of a mid-eighteenth-century Italian concert is recreated in an engraving by Giorgio Poggiali. As noble folk stroll about a palace, an orchestra and chorus, complete with organ, provide musical diversion from the gallery above.

devils had been at the instrument." Handel is said to have had "uncommon brilliancy and command of finger, but what distinguished him from all other players who possessed these same qualities was that amazing fullness, force, and energy which he joined with them."

Scarlatti was born in Naples but went to Lisbon in his mid-thirties and then spent the rest of his life in Spain as music master and harpsichordist to Maria Barbara de Braganza, afterward queen of Spain. Following the royal family on its rounds of the great palaces from Seville to Aranjuez, he composed some 550 harpsichord sonatas that are brief, incisive, and touched with some of the rhythmic fire of Spanish folk music. He could elaborate a musical idea more brilliantly in three minutes than anyone else in thirty—not, as he said, with profound intentions but as "an ingenious jesting in art."

Handel's muse wore a more serious mien: he preferred to fill whole evenings with his operas and oratorios. Born in Halle, in Saxony, he went to London for a visit in 1710 and liked it so well that he settled there permanently two years later. As "the Orpheus of our age" he became the principal purveyor of Italian opera to the English public, writing and producing dozens of operas with various companies in which he had a financial stake. Unlike Bach, who was tied to his jobs and children, Handel remained unmarried and self-employed, risking his own capital when he could not borrow from others and riding the seesaw of free enterprise in the cutthroat theatrical world of London. When his operas suddenly went out of style, leaving him with a bankrupt theater and a deficit equivalent to 150,000 dollars, he came close to serving a term in debtor's prison. He extricated himself only when it finally dawned on him that an English public might prefer English texts to Italian ones. Oratorios like *Saul, Israel in Egypt,* and *Solomon* helped him pay off his creditors and changed him from an embattled impresario into a dignified elder statesman of music.

Essentially, Handel's oratorios were Italian operas in disguise—biblical operas in English, shorn of scenery and action. Much of the love music he had written for his amorous operas was easily transferred to this "sacred" framework, and sounds equally valid in either context. Certainly there was no doubt that he had found the ideal medium for projecting the sweep and drama of the Scriptures. "Words are wanting to express the exquisite Delight it afforded to the admiring crowded Audience," reported the Dublin press after the 1742 première of his oratorio *Messiah.* "The Sublime, the Grand and the Tender, adapted to the most elevated, majestick and moving Words, conspired to transport and charm the ravished Heart and Ear." *Messiah* earned him a lasting place in the affections of the musical world, and smoothed his way into Westminster Abbey. When he was buried there in April, 1759, "There was almost the greatest Concourse of People of all Ranks ever seen upon such, or indeed upon any other Occasion."

4

Mozart's Europe

When Franz Joseph Haydn, aged twenty-nine, became conductor of Prince Esterházy's private orchestra in 1761, his contract stipulated, among other things, that he should "conduct himself as becomes an honorable official of a princely household," appear always in the prescribed uniform and wig, and inquire twice daily "whether His Highness is pleased to order a performance of the orchestra." The idea that this kind of servitude might be incompatible with his dignity as an artist never occurred to him. He worked for the Esterházy family for thirty years, and neither he nor his employers ever had cause to regret the arrangement.

By eighteenth-century standards Haydn was an immense success, having begun his career in an unheated garret and worked his way up to the rank of princely *Kapellmeister*. As head of what one of the princes called "the music individuals," he was on a par with the master of the stables and the keeper of the silver: "My prince was always satisfied with my works; I not only had the encouragement of constant approval, but as conductor of an orchestra I could make experiments, observe what produced an effect and what weakened it, and was thus in a position to improve, alter, make additions or omissions, and be as bold as I pleased. I was cut off from the world; there was no one to confuse or torment me, and I was forced to become *original*."

Haydn's principal task was to provide the musical entertainment at Esterháza, an immense pleasure palace built by Prince Nicholas, "the Magnificent," as a Hungarian rival to Versailles. His orchestra of about twenty men soon became renowned as one of the best in all of the Habsburg domains, and with it he proceeded to create a whole new world of instrumental music. Beginning modestly with orchestral works that still took the form of serenades or divertimenti (musical "diversions"), he gradually evolved the classical symphony with its four contrasting movements: allegro, adagio, minuet, finale.

Haydn composed a hundred-odd symphonies during his lifetime, and he never stopped experimenting with the symphony's possible form and contents. Sometimes he began with a long slow movement rather than the usual brilliant allegro; sometimes he employed shock effects and trick rhythms deliberately written to throw the listener off balance; sometimes he based whole movements on Hungarian or Croation folksongs or on complex contrapuntal forms. In the Symphony No. 60, the

The musical life of eighteenth-century England was enjoyably rich, attracting such continental musicians as Haydn, Mozart, and Handel for public performances. Music also played an integral role in home life, as the detail opposite from Johann Zoffany's painting of the Sharp family attests.

violins are required to mistune their lowest string from G down to F, then interrupt in mock horror and re-tune raucously. The Symphony No. 73, *La Chasse*, incorporates a dashing hunting episode from one of Haydn's operas. The *Farewell Symphony* (No. 45) was composed, so the story goes, because Prince Esterházy had taken to spending too much time in his drafty summer place, to which the musicians were not permitted to bring their families. In 1772, the prince so extended his season that the players became desperate to rejoin their wives and children. Haydn solved the problem diplomatically by composing a symphonic finale in which one player after another blew out his candle and departed, leaving only two violins to carry on to the end—presumably they were played by Haydn himself and his concertmaster, Tomasini, the prince's favorite. His Highness took the hint. "Well, if they all leave we might as well leave, too," he is reported to have said, and the court departed the next day.

Esterháza had its own band-box opera theater, for which Haydn wrote Italian operas in the fashion of the day. They made a lasting impression on the Empress Maria Theresa when she paid a gala visit to the palace in 1773. "If I want to hear a good opera I shall come to Esterháza," she declared afterward, a remark that must have given considerable satisfaction to the prince, who liked to boast that he could match the emperor in everything. He was one of the richest men in Europe, and the entertainments he provided for the empress were lavish

even by court standards. The Viennese newspapers reported that her visit was marked by an almost continual succession of musical delights. First she was offered a comic opera by Haydn, then an elaborate masked ball. "Later the empress was taken to the Chinese pavilion, whose mirror-covered walls reflected countless lanterns and chandeliers flooding the room with light. On a platform sat the princely orchestra in gala uniform and played under Haydn's direction his new symphony, entitled *Maria Theresa*, together with other music. The empress then retired to her magnificent suite, while her retinue continued to enjoy the ball until dawn."

The next day an enormous banquet took place, "during which the virtuosos of the orchestra demonstrated their skill." In the afternoon the empress attended a performance of Haydn's marionette opera, *Philemon et Baucis*. After supper the guests watched a huge display of fireworks arranged by the pyrotechnician Rabel, "their variety and brilliance surpassing all expectation." The visiting monarch was then conducted to an immense open space hung with multicolored lights. "Suddenly, about a thousand peasants appeared in their beautiful Hungarian and Croation costumes [since they were serfs, this was not an expensive production number], and performed national dances to the entrancing tunes of their own folk music. The next morning the empress left, after distributing costly presents. Haydn received a valuable golden snuffbox filled with ducats. . . ."

Life at Esterháza was not always so spectacular, however, and Haydn grew rather weary of the daily routine of serving on the household staff. What he really liked were the soirées in Vienna, where he could make chamber music with "people of my own class." He sometimes felt "forsaken in the wilderness" of the prince's estates. As he wrote to a Viennese lady in an *opera buffa* letter dated February 9, 1790, "Here in Esterháza no one asks me: 'Would you like some chocolate, with milk or without; will you take some coffee, black or with cream? What may I offer you, my dear Haydn? Would you like a vanilla or a pineapple ice?' "

Only a few months later, following the death of Prince Nicholas, Haydn suddenly found himself pensioned off at full pay and free to come and go as he pleased. Rather than retire in Vienna at fifty-eight, he elected to see something of the world. His young friend Wolfgang Amadeus Mozart, who had already toured all of Europe in his child-prodigy days, is said to have wept when he heard the news that Haydn had signed a contract to appear in London. "Do not go, Papa!" he pleaded. "You are not suited to the great world, and you speak so few languages." To which Haydn is said to have replied, "But the language I speak is understood the world over!"

Not the least of Haydn's reasons for leaving home was his desperate need to escape not only his tiresome wife but also his increasingly importunate mistress, the Italian singer Loisa Polzelli. A year of separation helped to cool off what was becoming a rather difficult situation. Ultimately she had to content herself with no more than a legal option on Haydn: "I, the undersigned, promise to Signora Loisa Polzelli (in case I should consider marrying again) to take no other wife than said Loisa Polzelli. . . ."

Safely arrived in London, Haydn was able for the first time to enjoy the fruits of his international fame. "Everyone wants to know me," he reported happily. "I had to dine out six times up to now, and if I wanted, I could dine out every day; but I must first consider my health, and second my work. Except for the nobility, I admit no callers till 2 o'clock in the afternoon." For Johann Peter Salomon, the concert promoter who had guaranteed the tour, he composed the twelve symphonies that constitute the capstone of his career—and are still the most often performed of all his symphonies. "At the concerts in Hanover Square where he has presided," wrote the noted English music critic Dr. Charles Burney, "his presence seems to have awakened such a

Old enough to be Mozart's father, Haydn befriended the young virtuoso in Vienna. In the imaginative engraving at right by Francis Rigaud, Haydn plays as Mozart listens—or makes notations on a score. An 1808 performance of Haydn's oratorio The Creation was immortalized in a watercolor painted on a golden snuff box that was presented to Haydn after the performance; the engraving below is based on that memento. All Vienna—including Beethoven—had turned out to greet the aged composer (seated at center).

degree of enthusiasm in the audience as almost amounts to frenzy."

Only one thing marred his well-deserved triumph: the news that, during his absence, Mozart had died in Vienna. "For some time I was beside myself about his death," he wrote to a mutual friend, "and I could not believe that Providence would so soon claim the life of such an indispensable man." Haydn had always recognized that here was a composer greater than himself: "Posterity," he declared, "will not see such a talent again in a hundred years!" And although after his return to Vienna, Haydn became the teacher of the young Beethoven, it may very well be that he was right. Certainly there has never been another native talent like Mozart's; as Sacheverell Sitwell put it, he was "the most gifted human being that has ever been born."

Hardly less remarkable, however, is the fact that Haydn, unlike the rest of his colleagues, was never jealous of this phenomenal young man. Instead, he did his best to tell the world about Mozart's genius. When, in 1787, someone wrote him from Prague asking him to write a comic opera, he recommended Mozart instead: "If I could impress on the soul of every friend of music, and on high personages in particular, how inimitable are Mozart's works, how profound, how musically intelligent, how extraordinarily sensitive! (for this is how I understand them, how I feel them)—why then the nations would vie with each other to possess such a jewel within their frontiers. ... It enrages me to think that this incomparable Mozart is not yet engaged by some imperial or royal

court! Forgive me if I lose my head: but I love the man so dearly. . . ."

Haydn had first met Mozart during one of Haydn's annual visits to Vienna, probably during the winter of 1781-82, when he was fifty and Mozart exactly half that age. Haydn's schedule did not permit them to spend much time together, but from that time on, the two were on the warmest terms of mutual admiration. Musically the example of one always stimulated the other, so that both wrote their best works after the start of their friendship. Between them they established most of the sonata and symphonic precedents that account for the lasting fame of the Viennese classical school. "Mozart was able, through the peculiar gift of his genius, effortlessly and suddenly to reach a level of symphonic perfection for which Haydn had struggled for decades," writes the Haydn scholar H. C. Robbins Landon. Mozart also learned a great deal from Haydn's string quartets, and as an expression of his gratitude, he dedicated six of his own to Haydn in 1785: the inscription addresses him, with almost filial affection, as "a highly celebrated man and my dearest friend." It was while they were trying out some of these quartets in Vienna that Haydn turned to Mozart's father and said, "I tell you before God and as an honest man that your son is the greatest composer I know, either personally or by reputation. . . ."

This unsolicited testimonial must have come as balm to the elder Mozart, a man full of wise counsels and dire prophesies (usually correct, but unheeded) about the consequences of his son's easygoing ways. Leopold Mozart was assistant conductor at the court of the prince-archbishop of Salzburg. He was an earnest, dedicated musician who was very much the dominant figure in his son's life. Mozart the *Wunderkind*, the child prodigy, had been to a large extent his invention. When he realized that he had a son with incredible gifts—a child who could play the piano like an adult, who had perfect pitch and an infallible memory for music—he decided that it was his obligation (and might also be profitable) "to convince the world of this miracle."

When Wolfgang was six, he and his gifted sister Nannerl were taken on the first of a long series of concert tours that were to cover most of the major courts in Western Europe. In Vienna Wolfgang was allowed to jump into Maria Theresa's ample lap; in France he played at Versailles and was offended when Madame de Pompadour refused his kisses; in England he was warmly received by George III and played fugues with Johann Christian Bach, the youngest of Bach's sons. "His execution was amazing," reported a British music lover who heard Mozart improvise on the piano when he was nine. "He was also a great master of modulation, and his transitions from one key to another were excessively natural and judicious. . . ."

This great knack for modulation was always one of the hallmarks of Mozart's style. If he was a "master" of the art at nine, he was a sheer miracle worker in later years, after he had developed a harmonic subtlety and breadth unequaled by any other composer. It is the modulations that account for the remarkable poignance of so much of Mozart's music, but these key changes are always very subtly prepared. Not for him are the sudden shocks and *volte-face* deceptions of Haydn's symphonies, and still less the "clumsy plunging" with which some of

At right Leopold Mozart plays the violin while his gifted young son Wolfgang performs at the harpsichord and his daughter Maria Anna (nicknamed Nannerl) sings. The Mozarts lived in the house above in Salzburg.

his lesser contemporaries peppered their works. He was always very critical of those who did not understand this art. "He modulates in such a violent way as to make you think he is resolved to drag you with him by the scruff of the neck," he wrote to his father after hearing the Mannheim composer Joseph Vogler. And again, when he first heard the music of Friedrich Graf in 1777: "He often plunged into a new key far too brusquely and it is all quite devoid of charm." To show how it ought to be done, Mozart then proceeded to give a practical demonstration. "Herr Graf, who is director here, stood transfixed, like someone who has always imagined his wanderings from key to key are quite unusual and now finds that one can be even more unusual and yet not offend the ear. In a word, they were all astounded." This was typical of the object lessons he used to give, very nonchalantly, while cutting a swath through the musical world. And then he wondered why he had so many jealous rivals.

Of all the stopping places on Mozart's grand tour, it was operatic Italy that gave him the greatest pleasure and recognition. In Rome he was decorated with the Order of the Golden Spur, although afterward he was unable to make use of his knighthood because the genuine aristocrats would not have tolerated a title acquired by a fluke. The venerable Philharmonic Academy of Bologna elected him to membership at

Seated at the harpsichord, Mozart is shown playing in Paris for the court of Prince Conti during one of his European tours. The tour, and others like it, failed to accomplish its aim—that of providing Wolfgang with a good musical post.

fourteen—the youngest musician in its history—after he had demonstrated his ability to write the most difficult sort of counterpoint. Better yet, his operas found favor with the hypercritical Milanese. Since he spoke Italian fluently, he felt very much at home there amid the frenetic bustle of music. In 1772 he wrote to his sister, who had remained in Salzburg: "Upstairs we have a violinist, downstairs another one, in the next room a singing master who gives lessons, and in the other room opposite ours an oboist. That is good fun when you are composing! It gives you plenty of ideas!"

Most musical prodigies begin to falter sometime late in adolescence and never regain their original momentum; it seems to take a special sort of tenacity to overcome the disadvantages of a too-spectacular head start in life. It was Mozart's well-developed sense of his own worth that carried him past the danger point in the cycle, when he was no longer young enough to be a prodigy but was merely a young man with a great deal of talent and no particular prospects. "I am a composer and was born to be a *Kapellmeister*," he wrote to his father, who had suggested he might earn a living by teaching, "and I neither can nor ought to bury the talent for composition with which God in his goodness has so richly endowed me (I may say so without conceit, for I feel it now more than ever). . . ."

But under the patronage system of musicmaking it was not easy to earn a living. The nobility had a stranglehold on the arts, and there was no place in their scheme of things for an impatient genius. "I am surrounded by mere brute beasts," he wrote from the heart of fashionable Paris, relating that the Duchesse de Chabot had kept him waiting for half an hour in an ice-cold, unheated room before condescending to appear for a private recital. Then she sat down with her friends and made drawings for another hour while "not only my hands but my whole body and my feet were frozen and my head began to ache." At last it was Mozart's turn to do what he had come for: "I played on that miserable, wretched pianoforte. But what vexed me most of all was that Madame and all her gentlemen never interrupted their drawing for a moment, but went on intently, so that I had to play to the chairs, tables and walls. Under these detestable conditions I lost my patience. I therefore began to play the Fischer variations and after playing half of them I stood up. Whereupon I received a shower of compliments."

Mozart's rebellious tendencies were not exactly helpful to an office seeker in the protocol-ridden eighteenth century, and he never found the powerful patron who might have smoothed the way for him. He had too little diplomacy for Paris, too little influence in Munich, and too many rivals in Vienna. For a time a stopgap solution was found for him in Salzburg, although the archbishop took a rather dim view of the prodigal returned. He was appointed court and cathedral organist at a salary of four hundred gulden per year, just below the poverty line. Life in Salzburg, moreover, was far too confining for Mozart's taste. "I detest Salzburg," he wrote to a friend, "and not only on account of the injustices which my dear father and I have endured there. . . . Salzburg is no place for my talent. In the first place, professional musicians are not held in much consideration; and secondly, one hears nothing, there is no theater, no opera; and even if they really wanted one, who is there to sing?"

His patience finally snapped when he was made to sit at the valets' table during one of the archbishop's state visits to Vienna. Their last interview terminated (as Mozart tells it) when the composer, assuming that the archbishop was not satisfied with him, questioned the prelate. In a fury, the archbishop replied: "What, you dare to threaten me—you scoundrel? There is the door! Look out, for I will have nothing more to do with such a miserable wretch." Mozart shot back, "Nor I with you," and the archbishop, having the final word, commanded, "Well, be off!"

From then on Mozart lived in Vienna as a freelance composer, giving concerts and piano lessons, and writing music on commission. His real greatness as a composer began precisely at the point where he turned his back on rococo etiquette and struck out into the uncharted regions of a subjective, utterly personal music. It was a quiet revolution, occurring almost secretly in the inner voices of his string quartets, the long, arching andantes of his piano concertos, and the breathtaking multiplicity of his operatic ensembles, in which several different characters, each expressing his own feelings, unite to form a perfect harmonic nexus that also sums up the dramatic situation of the moment. It

The portrait of Mozart at right by Taddeo Helbling shows the renowned prodigy at the age of eleven or twelve; it is considered one of the most faithful likenesses of the composer.

Overleaf: A party of gaily dressed Florentines enjoy a musical afternoon in this scene created from precious stones.

was a revolution of sensibility, and it accounts for the paradox that Mozart, the embodiment, if not the founder, of Viennese classicism, is also the one who sounds the first unmistakably romantic note.

Musical romanticism is a very difficult quality to define. It makes its first appearance in music like the slow movement of the Piano Concerto No. 21, with its gradual unfolding of a theme that takes a leisurely stroll down a chromatic staircase while the harmonies change, vibrantly, beneath it. This is the "dreamy and enchanting melancholy" that Stendhal found so fascinating in Mozart. But there is also a darker, more passionate side: the "terrifying anticipations of the Unspeakable" that the romantic poet E. T. A. Hoffmann (author of the fantastic *Tales*) heard in the overture to *Don Giovanni*, with its tremendous conflict "between the nature of man and cruel, unknown powers that lure him to destruction." What is particularly exciting about Mozart's later works is that the "speakable" and the "unspeakable" manage to get along so well together; he makes melancholy and laughter and life and death coexist in musical time-space. This chiaroscuro mixture, with its beautifully ambiguous effects, is one of Mozart's unique achievements. The nineteenth-century romantics tried for something similar, but never discovered the secret of his alloy: it is not enough merely to have saints and sinners on the same stage.

Mozart himself, according to his friends, was a chiaroscuro personality with a penchant for self-contradiction. Perhaps it had something to do with the fact that he was a very small man, with a frail physique

In the highly romanticized scene at left, below, Mozart is shown sitting in a room in the summer resort village of Josefsdorf near Vienna where he composed The Magic Flute; above is a reproduction of the front page of the first edition of Don Giovanni. Mozart composed the opera as a tribute to the city of Prague, which had acclaimed him and to which he had also dedicated The Marriage of Figaro.

but the temperament of a titan. "The expression on his face changed every moment, but indicated nothing more than the pleasure or pain which he experienced at the instant," recorded Heinrich von Schlichtegroll, who wrote his account with the help of Mozart's sister. "His body was perpetually in motion; he was either playing with his hands, or beating the ground with his foot."

The Irish tenor Michael Kelly (billed as "Signor Ochelly" when he sang the first Basilio in Mozart's *Marriage of Figaro* in 1796) writes in his reminiscences that Mozart was fond of punch and of billiards: "Many and many a game have I played with him, but always came off second best. He gave Sunday concerts, which I always attended. He was kindhearted, and always ready to oblige, but so very particular when he played that, if the slightest noise were made, he instantly left off."

Gradually, Mozart's music began to find an audience. *Figaro* made a name for him not only in Vienna but also in Prague, where it scored an instant success and earned him a commission for a new work, which turned out to be *Don Giovanni*. When he played the piano in Prague for the first time, following a performance of the *Prague Symphony*, composed especially for the concert, the audience could scarcely restrain itself. "Never before had there been such overwhelming and unanimous ecstasy as his divine playing aroused," wrote the Czech critic Franz Nemecek. "We truly did not know which we ought to admire the more, the extraordinary compositions or the extraordinary playing. Both together produced a total effect upon our souls which resembled a sweet enchantment."

Ultimately he obtained a small stipend as nominal composer to the imperial court. It was not enough, however, to end his chronic financial deficits, and he was forced to appeal to his friends for charity disguised as loans. During the summer of 1788, for example, while he was composing the last three magnificent symphonies (No. 39 in E Flat, No. 40 in G Minor, and No. 41 in C, the *Jupiter*) he did not earn enough money to pay the rent, and had to borrow repeatedly from his fellow Freemason Michael Puchberg. These troubles could not reach his music —the passionate discontent one hears expressed in the G Minor Symphony belongs to another order of anguish. But in the end they destroyed him physically.

Mozart died at thirty-five of what seems to have been rheumatic fever followed by a cardiac collapse. When he fell ill, he was hard at work, of course, on an unfinished requiem Mass that had been commissioned by an agent from an "unknown gentleman" whom Mozart instinctively recognized as the messenger of death. "On the day of his death," Nemecek records, "he had the score brought to his bed. 'Didn't I prophesy that I was writing this requiem for myself?' So he spoke and looked through the whole thing attentively once more with wet eyes. It was the last anguished look of parting from his beloved art."

5

Beethoven and His Century

THE NEW CENTURY BEGAN with great expectations. If there was one thing its young idealists could agree on it was their belief in the coming victory of humanity over tyranny and ignorance. The French Revolution had swept away the last detested remnants of the feudal system. "Europe at that time was thrilled with joy," wrote William Wordsworth in *The Prelude*, "France standing on the top of golden hours, and human nature seeming born again."

Clearly the time had come for privilege to give way to talent. And the heir to the revolution, Napoleon Bonaparte, seemed to personify the genius of the new age—a self-made Caesar who had won his empire on the strength of his abilities. As it turned out, however, he was soon subverting the very principles of liberty and fraternity that had smoothed his way to power. But not even the experience of the Napoleonic Wars, with their attendant miseries, could diminish the nineteenth century's optimism about the impending brotherhood of man. As John Keats expresses it in one of his sonnets:

> And other spirits are standing apart
> Upon the forehead of the age to come;
> These, these will give the world another heart,
> And other pulses. Hear ye not the hum
> Of mighty workings?—
> Listen awhile ye nations, and be dumb.

The musicians as well as the poets heard the hum of mighty workings. In the great chorale finale of Ludwig van Beethoven's Ninth Symphony, with its text based on Friedrich Schiller's *Ode to Joy*, the singers prophesy that "all men will become brothers beneath joy's gentle wing," and the movement reaches its climax at the words with which Schiller (and with him, Beethoven) proclaims his capacious love for the whole of mankind: *Seid umschlungen, Millionen!*—"Be embraced, ye millions! Take this kiss for all the world!" This is an extraordinary message to appear within the framework of a symphony, and it could only be the product of a heroic time in literature and the arts. Never again were such sentiments to be expressed with such freshness, power, and conviction, and in music that is so perfectly attuned to the spirit of its time. Nor was there any other composer who articulated so clearly the whole romantic quest for freedom, energy, and grandeur. "With

Beethoven's energy and fiery passion emerge in this engraving taken from a romanticized portrait by Joseph Karl Stieler; the brooding composer holds the score of his Missa Solemnis, *an awe-inspiring work of 1823.*

75

Beethoven," wrote the great pianist and composer Ferruccio Busoni, "humanity enters into music for the first time."

The first performance of Beethoven's Ninth Symphony, on May 7, 1824, was a milestone in the annals of music, and eyewitness accounts of it tell us a great deal about Beethoven's position in the musical world of his day. The symphony had been finished, after five years of intermittent labor, toward the end of 1823, but Beethoven was uncertain about where to present the première until a group of his Viennese friends presented him with a petition couched in the most flattering terms. Describing themselves as "reverent admirers" of his genius, they pleaded with him not to keep them waiting any longer for his latest composition. "We know that a new flower glows in the garland of your glorious, still unequaled symphonies," they wrote, arguing that the honor of the première should go to Vienna, "for though Beethoven's name and creations belong to all contemporaneous humanity and every country which opens a susceptible bosom to art, it is Austria which is best entitled to claim him as her own." The petition contained thirty signatures, among them the city's leading music publishers and instrument makers, several officials of the imperial court, and a dozen prominent aristocrats, headed by Prince Carl Lichnowsky, Count Czernin, the first chamberlain of the emperor, and Count Moritz Dietrichstein, the director of court theaters.

Beethoven was not easily persuaded, but at last he consented to give a "grand musical academy" (as concerts were then called) in one of the court theaters—the Kärntnerthor Theater. Since there was no professional orchestra available (the Vienna Philharmonic was not founded until 1842), he followed his usual practice of recruiting an orchestra especially for the occasion. In modern parlance this would be called a "pick-up group." It consisted of his friends among the stringplayers of the city, members of the most prominent amateur organization, the

Beethoven's early recognition came as a result of his virtuoso playing of the piano; a pen sketch above shows him standing fingering a keyboard. Eventually Beethoven was lionized as a composer, and his works, published by the house of Artaria (seen in the view at left of the Kohlmarkt in Vienna), were presented all over Europe. The watercolor below, contemporaneous with Beethoven, shows a concert in an ornate Milan hall.

Musikfreunde, or "friends of music," and professional players from the Kärntnerthor Theater orchestra. The chorus was wholly amateur, and one of his assistants was moved to complain that "the women's choir is not of the best because they are all very young girls."

As soprano and alto soloists, fortunately, he had two seasoned professional singers, Henriette Sontag and Caroline Unger, who had befriended him two years before. ("Two singers visited me today," he had written to his brother on the day of their first meeting, in 1822, "and since they wanted by all means to kiss my hands and were really pretty, I proposed that they kiss my mouth.") "The beautiful witches," as Beethoven called them, continued to cultivate his friendship, and Caroline, particularly, had been one of the most ardent supporters of the projected première. Yet once the vocal rehearsals had started, she could not refrain from telling Beethoven that she thought her part too demanding and that he was "a tyrant over all vocal chords." Beethoven replied, in a rare good humor, that the two ladies had been spoiled by singing too much Italian opera. "But these high notes here, couldn't they be changed?" Henriette Sontag persisted. Beethoven refused to change a note of what he had written. "Oh, all right! Let's struggle on with it for God's sake," the soprano finally conceded, and apparently both women learned to cope with the high tessitura without straining their voices (just as all subsequent singers of the Ninth have done).

A good deal of "hellish confusion" is said to have reigned during the preparations for the concert. The bass soloist had to be replaced at the last minute; at the eleventh hour an assistant noted that the chorus

singers "still don't know a single note." To make matters worse, Beethoven could get these diverse forces together for only two rehearsals. Yet he was so pleased with the second rehearsal that afterward he stood at the door embracing the many volunteers who donated their services.

Under the circumstances, the performance itself went surprisingly well. The orchestra was more than double the usual size—twenty-four violins, ten violas, twelve cellos and contrabasses, and twice the usual number of wind players. Beethoven himself stood at the conductor's desk, but he had three assistants: one to lead the choir, another to beat time among the violins, and a third to reinforce the rhythm at the piano (no conductor today would dare to add a piano, ad lib, to the orchestral texture of the Ninth).

First violinist Josef Böhm described the composer's excitement during the performance: "Beethoven moved back and forth like a man possessed. Sometimes he stretched high into the air, sometimes he cowered close to the ground; he flailed the air with his hands and feet as though he wanted to play all the instruments himself, and to sing all of the mighty chorus." But the musicians wisely watched only the baton in the hands of the assistant conductor, Ignaz Umlauf. "Beethoven was so excited that he did not notice what was going on around him," nor was he aware of the tremendous applause and shouts of enthusiasm that greeted the end of the performance. "Then it was that Caroline Unger had the presence of mind to turn the master towards the proscenium and show him the cheering crowd throwing their hats into the air and waving their handkerchiefs." The startled expression on his face, "and the sudden conviction thereby forced on everybody that *he could not hear what was going on* acted like an electric shock on all present, and a volcano of sympathy and admiration erupted."

Beethoven by then had been suffering from ear trouble for more than twenty-five years, and had been acutely deaf for nearly half of that time. According to modern medical opinion, his illness was probably caused by the aftereffects of a severe attack of typhoid fever in his youth. Its influence on his life and work are immeasurable: "My whole life has been poisoned," he said, by this almost inconceivable handicap. As it was he spent half of his life in a titanic struggle for his continued existence as a composer. "I must live in exile," he wrote to his brothers in a confessional letter, the so-called Heiligenstadt Testament of 1802. "What humiliation when someone stood next to me and heard a flute in the distance and I heard *nothing*, or when someone heard the *shepherd boy singing*, and I again heard nothing. Such misfortunes brought me to the edge of despair, and I might have brought an end to my life— only my art held me back. Oh, it seemed impossible for me to quit this world until I had produced everything I felt I could produce."

Beethoven's deafness cut him off from the world and gave him a reputation as a *Menschenhasser*, a "misanthrope"; yet at the same time it had much to do with focusing his attention on the purely ideal and conceptual elements of his art. A composer who can hear no music except what he can project in his aural imagination has no use for trivia or the conventions of virtuoso musicmaking. Having overcome his handicap by sheer will power, he was less and less concerned with the

The houses in which Beethoven spent his first and last days are shown opposite. The one above is the house in Vienna where he died in 1827; the view below shows the interior of his father's house in Bonn. It was from this house that the seventeen-year-old Beethoven journeyed to Vienna to play for Mozart (an event re-created in the illustration above); although Mozart was impressed, little good came of the trip.

workaday aspects of practical music. "Do you believe that I think of your miserable fiddle when the Spirit dictates and I write it down?" he asked "Milord" Schuppanzigh, the first violinist of the quartet for whom he composed many of his chamber works. And when Felix Radicati, a violinist who helped him with the fingering of the so-called Rasoumovsky Quartets, had the temerity to tell him, "Surely you do not consider these works as music," Beethoven replied confidently, "Oh, they are not for you, but for a later age!"

His professional colleagues, with their traditionalist notions about what was fitting and proper in music, tended to be very patronizing toward him. His works sounded so strange to their ears that they sincerely believed that deafness had unhinged his mind. One of the more distinguished composers of the day, Louis Spohr, wrote that Beethoven's "aesthetic aberrations" must have been caused by his illness. Once he could no longer hear any music, "his constant endeavor to be original and to open new paths could no longer, as formerly, be preserved from error by the guidance of his ear. Was it then to be wondered at that his works became more and more eccentric, unconnected and incomprehensible?" When Spohr visited Beethoven and heard him vainly hammering away at the keyboard without being able to hear what he was playing, he remarked, "I felt moved with the deepest sorrow at so hard a destiny. It is a sad misfortune for anyone to be

deaf; how then should a musician endure it without despair? Beethoven's almost continual melanchony 'was no longer a riddle to me now."

It had been a very different matter in the mid-1790's when Beethoven first arrived in Vienna to become the young lion of the salons. As chamber musician to the relatively modest court of Bonn, his birthplace, he had already established an enviable reputation as a pianist. But it was among the music-loving nobility of Vienna that he came into his own as a "giant among pianists" who possessed a technique and an imagination "beyond anything which we might have dreamed." It was the golden age of the musical amateur, and once the Viennese music lovers had discovered the full dimensions of his genius, he was treated like a god descended from Olympus. Indeed the times had changed. Not for Beethoven were the long hours of waiting in drafty antechambers, like Mozart, until the great nobles would condescend to hear him play. On the contrary, it was he who kept *them* waiting. A French baron who tried to get an introduction to him in Vienna was told that it was impossible to arrange: "And to give you an idea of how little respect he has for conventions, let me tell you that the empress asked him one morning to call on her; he replied that he was busy all that day, but would try to look her up on the following one."

Understandably enough, his teacher, Joseph Haydn, nicknamed him "The Great Mogul." According to the aristocratic Frau von Bernhard, who heard him play in the palaces of Vienna when she was a young woman, his manners were those of a bear rather than a lion:

When he came to visit us, he would usually stick his head through the door to make sure no one was present whom he disliked. He was short and insignificant looking, with an ugly red face full of pock marks. His hair was very dark and hung almost shaggily about his face; his suit very ordinary, and in strong contrast to the fastidious elegance customary in those days. . . . He was very proud, and I have known him to refuse to play even when Countess Thun, the mother of Princess Lichnowsky, had fallen on her knees before him, as he sat on the sofa, to beg him to play.

Clearly the Viennese loved music more than good manners. To keep Beethoven from leaving the city (Bach, in similar circumstances, had simply been put under arrest), three prominent amateurs agreed to guarantee him a lifetime income of 4,000 gulden (about 15,000 dollars in today's terms) so long as he remained in Vienna. They were Prince Josef Lobkowitz, who played music from dawn to dusk with his private quartet; Prince Ferdinand Kinsky, a colonel in the Austrian army who had a passion for vocal music; and Archduke Rudolph, a half-brother of the reigning emperor and an excellent pianist, having studied piano and composition with Beethoven himself.

To hear Beethoven improvise at the piano was considered a great and unpurchasable privilege. His pupil Carl Czarny has testified to his technique:

> His improvisation was brilliant and astonishing in the extreme, and no matter in what company he might be, he knew how to make such an impression on every listener that frequently there was not a single dry eye, while many broke out in loud sobs, for there was a certain magic in his expression. . . . When he had concluded an improvisation of this kind, he was capable of breaking out into boisterous laughter and of mocking his listeners for the emotion he had called forth in them. He would even say to them, "You are fools!" At times he felt himself insulted by such manifestations of sympathy. "Who can continue to live among such spoiled children?" he would cry. . . .

A Fragonard painting (left, above) shows an interlude of chamber music played by an ensemble containing a harp, French horn, flute, and violin. Beethoven (above, as imagined by an Italian artist) composed for small groups as well as for single instruments, but he is most widely admired for his implementation of the full orchestra.

Although he may have scorned their tears, he came to share their romantic conception of the composer as a man with a priestlike vocation. "Music is a higher revelation than all wisdom and philosophy," he is supposed to have told Bettina Brentano, the fascinating literary adventuress who befriended both Goethe and Beethoven. "Music is the wine which inspires one to new generative processes, and I am Bacchus who presses out this glorious wine for mankind and makes them spiritually drunken." This is in its very essence the German romantic view of music, shared by virtually all the poets and novelists involved in the German literary revolution between 1790 and 1830. One of the leading poets of the day, E. T. A. Hoffmann, described music as "the most romantic of all the arts; one could almost say the only purely romantic one, for its only model is the infinite. . . . Music unlocks for man an unknown realm, a world that has nothing in common with the world of the senses that surrounds him."

Hoffmann wrote many influential essays on the symphonies and operas of his time, and he became one of Beethoven's earliest literary champions—although almost everything he said about him is tinged with the customary romantic hyperbole, or so-called *Schwärmerei*. Beethoven's music, he wrote in his review of the Fifth Symphony, in 1810, "moves the lever of terror, of fear, of shock, of suffering, and it awakens that endless *Sehnsucht* [longing] which is the essence of romanticism."

The nineteenth-century poets always spoke of Beethoven in these terms; they persisted in seeing him in their own image. Yet he was not nearly so involved in "the realm of the unfathomable and the immeasurable," as they liked to believe. Despite his romantic conduct, Beethoven always remained something of an eighteenth-century rationalist (and not only on account of his dates, 1770-1827). Having "received the spirit of Mozart from the hands of Haydn" as one of his friends expressed it, he never abandoned the classical love of form he had inherited from his Viennese predecessors. It was a matter of his expanding and adapting, rather than demolishing, their elegant sonata forms. Hence the eternal confusion in the reference books as to whether he belongs among the "classic" or the "romantic" composers—an unnecessary distinction, in any event, since his range was so enormous that he was perfectly capable of embracing both.

Goethe, who wrote the most important book of the nineteenth century—*Faust*—is just as impossible to classify. His Faust, of course, is a man of infinite contradictions, a sensualist-intellectual—"Two souls

live, *Ach!* within my breast!"—and this implicit tension is characteristic of all of Goethe's writing. Beethoven's work, too, is Janus faced, looking backward with the logic and lucidity of the eighteenth century and forward with the heaven-storming passion of the nineteenth. Moreover, his music incorporates the whole arsenal of images and ideas that succeeding generations were to develop in their own fashion. His nine symphonies, sixteen string quartets, and thirty-two piano sonatas were to acquire a kind of canonical authority as definitive models—and unattainable ideals. "To us musicians," wrote Franz Liszt in 1852, "the work of Beethoven parallels the pillars of smoke and fire which led the Israelites through the desert, a pillar of smoke and fire to lead us by day and a pillar of fire to light the night, so that we may march ahead both day and night. His darkness and light equally trace for us the road we must follow; both the one and the other are a perpetual commandment, an infallible revelation."

It proved to be, however, an overpowering and frequently oppressive influence, although not until the end of the century did anyone dare to break the spell that Beethoven had cast over symphonic music. Claude Debussy, who was the first to do so, wrote an essay in which he suggested that Beethoven had exhausted the forms in which he worked and that his example ought therefore to be avoided. Proof of "the futility of the symphony" after Beethoven had been furnished by Robert Schumann and Felix Mendelssohn, who "did no more than respectfully repeat the same forms with less power." This is an unflattering but accurate view of what actually happened to the German tradition in the post-Beethoven era. Indeed, Mendelssohn, the "bright, pure, aspiring spirit" who wrote most of his finest music before he was eighteen, abandoned his airy *Midsummer Night's Dream* brilliance in order to assume the portentous attitude of the Beethoven symphonies. It was a pose so little suited to his real personality that, of his later works, only his chamber music fulfills his early promise. "He began by being a genius and ended by being a talent," was one conductor's unkind but succinct way of summing up the case.

Schumann also paid his debt to Beethoven by writing four magisterial and rather pompous symphonies, although his real genius was for small, lyrical forms like the fantasy pieces that make up the *Carnaval* suite for piano, or the *Kreisleriana* suite, inspired by a character in Hoffmann's *Tales*. If there is such a thing as a quintessential product of German musical romanticism (as opposed to the later and more radical French kind), then it is the poetry of Heinrich Heine set to music by Schumann, notably the *Dichterliebe* ("Poet's Love") and *Liederkreis* ("Garland of Songs") collections. As Schumann explained, such poems had inspired a whole new genre of music, "and thus arose that more artistic and profound style of song of which earlier composers could of course know nothing, for it was due to the new spirit of poetry reflected in music."

Of all the composers in this group, it was Franz Schubert who was best able to hold his own against the full force of the Beethoven tide—Schubert, who had lived all of his thirty-one years in Beethoven's shadow. Perhaps it was just as well that they were introduced to each other only at the very end of Beethoven's life, in 1827; had it been earlier, Schubert might have become just another one of Beethoven's many musical errand boys. As it was, he was able to develop a personal style that somehow managed to absorb the older composer's influence without being crushed by it. The generation gap had something to do with it. Schubert was twenty-seven years younger than Beethoven, and he moved in far less rarified social circles. His Viennese friends were the Bohemian poets, the young painters, the government clerks and merchants' daughters. He began his career as a schoolmaster and ended it a decade later as an unemployed composer of vast amounts of music, most of it unpublished. During his lifetime the Viennese publishers accepted only one of his nineteen quartets, only three of his twenty-one piano sonatas, one of his seven Masses, less than a third of his six hundred songs, and not a single one of his nine symphonies.

Only once in his life, in the spring of 1828, did Schubert give a concert of his own music—and it was prompted not by a petition of princes but by a letter from a friend who was a lawyer and would-be poet. "Do you want my advice?" wrote Eduard von Bauernfeld, "Every new song of yours is an event. You have composed the most glorious string quartets and trios, not to mention the symphonies. Your friends are enchanted with them, but as yet no publisher will buy them, and the public still has no idea of the beauty and grace that slumber in these works. So take a running start, master your inertia, give a concert. . . . A single evening will at least be enough to cover your expenses for a whole year." Schubert complied with the suggestion. His admirers rallied to the occasion and contributed their services, the *Musikfreunde* donated their hall free of charge, and the concert, consisting of songs, choruses, and chamber music, turned out to be a great success, netting the composer a profit of eight hundred gulden. With the proceeds he was at last able to buy himself a much-needed piano.

When it was suggested that he give a repeat performance, Schubert declined. He was not a concert virtuoso but a chamber player, a composer of choral serenades to be sung under girls' windows by moon-

light, a pianist who liked to play for his friends' parties. "He never danced," recalled his friend Leopold von Sonnleithner, "but he was always ready to sit down at the piano, where for hours he improvised the most beautiful waltzes; those he liked he repeated, in order to remember them and write them out afterwards. Mozart and especially *Beethoven* were his ideals . . . about them he became enthusiastic."

Sonnleithner testifies that Schubert was too retiring and tonguetied to venture out into the fashionable world: "He was only really animated among intimate friends. . . . He was shy and taciturn, especially in smart society, which he only frequented in order to accompany his songs, more or less as a favor. Whilst doing this his face wore the most serious expression, and as soon as it was over he withdrew into the neighboring room." Schubert was an even smaller man than Beethoven, and cut such an unprepossessing figure that his friends called him *Schwammerl*—"little mushroom." "Inwardly a poet and outwardly a kind of hedonist," he had a round face, stubby nose, short neck, bushy eyebrows, and thick curly hair—"one could have taken him for an Austrian, or more likely, a *Bavarian* peasant."

Yet there is no music that is lighter on its feet than Schubert's. And while Beethoven was at work putting the finishing touches to his epic tonal monuments, Schubert was busy inventing the German Lied, the epitome of all that was most lyrical in the romantic movement. There had been German songs before Schubert, but they lacked the unmistakable spark that, in his magnificent Lieder, is struck when the hammer of music meets the anvil of poetry. For him the text of a song often serves merely as a point of departure for some superb musical metaphors, and

The first generation of romantics after Beethoven were all principally composers for the piano: Mendelssohn (left, above), Robert Schumann (above), and Franz Schubert, seen in the idealized 1826 painting below playing at a musicale in his publisher's home. Schubert's intense admirers include Beethoven (who leans toward him over the piano), although Beethoven had long been acutely deaf; two years later both he and Schubert were dead.

many of his verses are by minor poets who would hardly rate one star in a guidebook to literary Germany. His best-known cycle, for example, *Die Schöne Müllerin* ("The Miller's Beautiful Daughter") is based on a group of sentimental verses by the otherwise undistinguished poet Wilhelm Müller. But to a composer accustomed to transcending his material, they were enough to inspire a series of brilliant character studies.

The piano always played a vital role in Schubert's songs, and in the *Müllerin* he has the accompaniment impersonating the millstream that "fumes and frets and foams" through the entire cycle, underscoring the turbulent emotions of its protagonists. Where the poet hears "a stream gushing from its rocky bed," Schubert has a flood of undulating figures in the accompaniment. And when, in the next song, the stream's power is harnessed to the mill wheel, the pages bear clusters of notes that look as if they were churning up a spray. Farther downstream is a place where, in a melancholy interlude, the hero sheds a tear or two; they can be heard splashing like raindrops in the accompaniment.

Famous for more than six hundred love songs and ballads, Schubert (left) gained inspiration from folk tunes, and as depicted in the scene at right, frequently listened to Gypsy musicmakers. In 1814 Vienna welcomed Europe's most important statesmen to a peace congress and feted them with song and dance, especially the popular waltz, as demonstrated by the willowy couple at left, below.

Beethoven, of course, never got to hear Schubert's songs, but he did get to see them when he was already in bed with his last illness. His factotum, Anton Schindler, brought him a collection of sixty Schubert Lieder, many of them still in manuscript. Schindler has described Beethoven's reaction:

> The master was amazed at the number of them, and simply could not believe that at that time [February, 1827] Schubert had already written over five hundred. But if he was amazed at their number, he was utterly astonished when he got to know their content. For several days he simply could not tear himself away from them, and he spent hours every day over *Iphigenia's Monologue*, *Grenzan der Menschheit*, *Die Allmacht*, *Die Junge Nonne*, *Viola*, the *Muller* Lieder, and others as well. With delighted enthusiasm he called out repeatedly, "Truly, in Schubert there dwells a divine spark!"

Schindler finally brought Schubert to Beethoven's bedside a week before his death. Nothing is known about what passed between them, except that when Beethoven was told that there were several visitors waiting to see him, he said, "Let Schubert come first!"

Schubert's friend Josef von Spaun has another story to tell that may help to explain why, until that moment, Schubert had always been too shy to approach Beethoven. One day, as Schubert was performing some of his songs for Spaun, he turned to his friend and asked, "Do you really think something will come of me?" Spaun was deeply moved, and as he later recalled, "I embraced him and said, 'You have done much already and time will enable you to do much more and great things, too.' Then he said quite humbly, 'Secretly, in my heart of hearts, I still hope to be able to make something out of myself, but who can do anything after Beethoven?' "

6

The Romantic Imagination

PARIS IN THE EARLY 1830's was "the capital of the nineteenth century" —a city of poets, painters, and musicians, of brilliant young men with daring ideas and abundant energies for carrying them out: Alexandre Dumas, Alfred de Musset, Théophile Gautier, Alfred de Vigny, Honoré de Balzac, Prosper Mérimée, Gérard de Nerval. At the première of Victor Hugo's play *Hernani* in 1830, the clean-shaven supporters of classical conventions had been routed by the bearded partisans of romanticism. With the success of that theatrical coup d'état, the way was suddenly open for a new freedom of expression in every branch of the arts. "We were mad with lyricism and with art," Gautier remembered afterward. "It seemed as if we had just discovered a long-lost secret; and that was true, for we had rediscovered poetry."

It was an age to compare with the Italian Renaissance, a great cultural transformation based on a revolution of human consciousness. Not only poetry had been rediscovered by the romantics, but also the uses of history and myth, the beauties of nature in the Alps and the Mediterranean, and—not least—the psychic and sexual mysteries of the self. The Baroness Aurore Dudevant, better known to literature as George Sand, launched a great campaign for woman's liberation with her novels *Valentine, Indiana,* and *Lélia,* soon to be followed by still other passionate revelations about the true state of a woman's heart. Among the older writers, Stendhal, "the first *modern* man," published his masterpiece, *The Red and the Black,* in 1830. It is a ruthlessly unsentimental study of ambition and sexuality in a young man who has been described as the quintessential romantic hero, "a Napoleon without a sword." Henrich Heine came to Paris from Germany in 1831 to write some of the finest poetry and some of the most biting political satires of the age—"standing all alone," as Ford Madox Ford describes him, "perhaps the most exquisite of all the world's lyricists since the great Greeks, perhaps the greatest of all the world's realistic-bitter romantics."

The young painter Eugène Delacroix, newly returned from a voyage to North Africa, was already at work on the turbulent pictures of Arab life whose dazzling colors were to change the course of modern painting. His older rival Jean Auguste Ingres, meanwhile, continued to paint his cool, restrained portraits and neoclassical nudes. Stylistically these artists were poles apart, yet each in his own fashion was a thoroughly romantic artist.

On the musical scene, three young titans made their debuts within a few years of one another—Hector Berlioz, Franz Liszt, and Frédéric Chopin. The twenty-seven-year-old Berlioz stood Paris on its ear in that same fateful year of revolutions and turning points, 1830, when he presented the première of his *Symphonie fantastique*, an event that proclaimed the beginning of a new musical epoch. It also marked the start of his friendship with Liszt, who expressed his admiration for the *Fantastique* by making a piano arrangement of it which he played at his concerts and undertook to publish at his own expense.

Born in Hungary, Liszt had first come to Paris as a child prodigy. Now, as a virtuoso in his early twenties, he was giving the musical world a series of breathtaking demonstrations of what could be done with ten fingers on the eighty-eight keys of a pianoforte. Chopin, in his turn, came to Paris from Poland in 1831, when he was twenty-one, to demonstrate a keyboard technique and a style of composition that was more intimate and subtle than Liszt's. "Yes, one must grant Chopin genius in the fullest sense of the word," Heine wrote. "He is not simply a technician, he is a poet and can express for us the poetry that lives in his soul; he is a poet in sound, and nothing is quite like the delights he lavishes on us when he sits at the keyboard and improvises."

It was Berlioz, the eldest and also the most energetic of the three, who pointed the way for the others. Gifted, audacious, and fiercely devoted to his art, he possessed "the most powerful musical brain in France," as Liszt observed, and at the same time one of the best literary minds in the country. He loved literature of great themes and passions —Vergil, Byron, and above all, "Shakespeare and Goethe, the mute witnesses to my torments, who have explained my whole life to me." Some of his greatest works were inspired by *Romeo and Juliet, Faust, Childe Harold*, and *The Aeneid*. Yet it was not so much a matter of "illustrating" these works as of realizing his visions of them in sound—of finding their equivalents in the metaphor of music. That meant creating new forms or putting old ones to new uses. For *Romeo and Juliet* he devised the dramatic symphony, for *Faust* the dramatic legend (a kind of opera for the imagination), and for *The Tempest* and *King Lear* the dramatic overture or fantasia, which is really a kind of tone poem in classical disguise.

Liszt and Chopin were accustomed to working out their compositions at the piano; Berlioz always conceived of his music orchestrally from the very first. As a boy in provincial France he had studied flute and guitar rather than the piano (there happened to be none in his parents' home), and in later years he realized that this circumstance had shaped his whole approach to music. "When I consider the appalling platitudes to which the piano has given birth, I give grateful thanks to the good fortune that forced me to compose freely and in silence, and delivered me from the tyranny of the fingers, so dangerous to thought."

When he went to Paris, supposedly to become a doctor like his father, his passion for music made a change of plans inevitable. Before long, much against his family's wishes, he enrolled as a student of composition at the Conservatoire. He also became notorious as a heckler at the Paris Opéra, taking it upon himself to serve as a one-man watchdog

Hector Berlioz (above, as drawn by Ingres) was born in 1803, before the poet Goethe had completed his seminal work Faust. *Twenty-five years later Berlioz had composed* Eight Scenes from Faust *and in 1846 came his fully developed "imaginary opera"* The Damnation of Faust *(the program for the first performance is above, right). Berlioz' novel technique appeared earlier in his* Symphonie fantastique, *for which he published pre-performance program notes; a page from that symphony is shown below. The drawing at right, below, is of the showman violinist Nicolò Paganini, for whom Berlioz composed* Harold in Italy.

committee on behalf of his favorite composers, Gluck and Weber. The playwright Ernest Legouvé recalled afterward how he had caught his first glimpse of Berlioz at a performance of Weber's *Der Freischütz*. "Suddenly in the middle of the ritornello of Caspar's aria, one of my neighbors leaps to his feet, leans over to the orchestra and shouts in a thundering voice: 'Not two flutes, you scoundrels! Two piccolos! Two piccolos! Oh, what brutes!' "

It was Berlioz, in the full flowering of his wrath—and surely the only man in Paris who knew or cared that the orchestra was not following the score. Legouvé gives a memorable account of how he looked at that arch-romantic moment: "a young man quivering with rage, his hands clenched, eyes flashing, and an amazing head of hair, but what a head of hair! It was like an immense umbrella of hair, overhanging and waving about the beak of a bird of prey. It was comic and diabolical at the same time."

While he was still a student at the Conservatoire, an English theatrical troupe came to Paris to perform a season of Shakespeare. Berlioz promptly fell in love, not only with the plays, but with Harriet Smithson, the Irish actress who played Juliet and Ophelia. "It prostrated me, and my heart and whole being were invaded by a cruel, maddening passion, in which the love of a great artist and the love of a great art were mingled together, each intensifying the other." For a long time this terrible passion was to remain altogether unrequited. But fortunately the romantics were always at their best in the midst of a tempestuous love affair; their whole aesthetic movement depended for its power on just such an intermingling of art and sexuality.

True to form, Berlioz poured his feelings into the *Symphonie fantastique*, with its semiautobiographical scenario about a lovesick musician who tries to poison himself with opium, and sees his beloved in a series of feverish visions. Not until the second performance, in 1832, did Berlioz have an opportunity to invite Miss Smithson to hear the work. When the actress took her seat for the concert, she may have been the only person in the audience unaware that she herself figured as the heroine of the symphony, for she had heard only rumors of Berlioz' infatuation. Still, as he writes in his memoirs, "the passionate character of the work, its burning melodies, its cries of love, its accesses of fury, and the violent vibrations of such an orchestra heard close by, were bound to produce an impression."

Indeed, the message was unmistakable. Harriet went home in a trance; within the year they were married at the British embassy, with Liszt as witness. Not that there was to be a genuine fairy-tale ending to this most romantic of love stories. In time, Harriet became an alcoholic, and Berlioz left her to live with a young singer, Marie Recio, whom he was to marry after Harriet's death. But the first years following his marriage were easily the happiest and most productive of his life. He wrote *Harold in Italy* for that formidable virtuoso Nicolò Paganini (Heine called him "a vampire with a violin"), who became one of Berlioz' greatest admirers. The day after hearing *Harold* for the first time, Paganini sent the composer a gift of 20,000 francs, together with the note: "Beethoven is dead, and only Berlioz can revive his spirit!"

Thanks to this act of generosity, Berlioz was able to compose his great symphony with voices, *Romeo and Juliet*. "I worked for seven months at my symphony, not leaving off for more than three or four days out of every thirty on any pretence whatever. And during all that time, how ardently did I live!"

This ardor is one of the hallmarks of his whole life and style. Berlioz himself said that the dominant qualities of his music were "passionate expression, inner fire, rhythmic drive and the element of surprise." All of these were elements that distinguish the romantics' ideal from the orderly, positive, and more predictable manner of the classicists who preceded them. In performance, Berlioz added, his works required a very difficult combination of "extreme precision and irresistible verve, a regulated vehemence, a dreamy tenderness and an almost morbid melancholy."

These paradoxical features of musical romanticism are nowhere more in evidence than in the great *Requiem Mass*, which the French government commissioned him to write in 1837. Alfred de Vigny, after hearing the première, called it "beautiful and bizarre, savage, convulsive and heart-rending." It also gave Berlioz an unfortunate reputation as something of a circus ringmaster specializing in colossal effects and oversize orchestrations. In the *Dies Irae* ("Days of Wrath") section of the *Mass*, where the text speaks of the Last Judgment, Berlioz harnesses the power of massed voices and brasses to conjure up a spine-chilling vision of the trumpet call that will reverberate through the tombs of the dead. Here the main orchestra and chorus are surrounded by four satellite brass bands that challenge and answer one another in furious vectors of sound. It is an arrangement requiring split-second coordination, and Berlioz was never more in his element than when he had a chance to conduct this prophecy of the Apocalypse. His memoirs contain an account that gives us an inkling of the physical sensations he could experience on such occasions:

> The chorus sustained the assault of the orchestra without flinching; the fourfold peal of trumpets broke forth from the four corners of the stage, already vibrating with the rolling of ten kettledrums and the tremolo of fifty bows; and, in the midst of this cataclysm of sinister harmonies and noise from the other world, hurled forth their terrible prediction. . . .

He always responded physically to music, and on the podium he would sometimes be overcome by a sort of rapture of the deeps, what he described as "a peal of bells in my heart, a millwheel in my head, my knees knocking against each other." The great tragedy of his life was that he could not get enough of such experiences, for the music industry of Paris had no appropriate place for a man of his genius. When both of his grand operas proved to be failures, and the main orchestras, run by his rivals, turned a deaf ear to his works, he was forced to earn his living by writing music criticism for the newspapers. It was a job he detested, although he did it brilliantly, with more style and gusto than any critic before or since. To bring his own works before the public he had to become an impresario, hiring the hall and paying the musicians

The Shakespearean actress Harriet Smithson (left) fared little better than the Juliet or Ophelia she played; eventually courted by neither the public nor her husband, Berlioz, she turned to alcohol. Berlioz is caricatured below as the rather foppish conductor of his own music.

out of his own pocket. The one advantage of this arrangement was that, while composing, he was not bound to the dimensions of any existing orchestra. He could write for any orchestral combination that suited his particular purpose, and for the acoustics of the hall in which the performance would occur.

The problem of acoustic balance is a technical question, but a highly significant one, since it arose directly out of the social and economic changes accompanying the Industrial Revolution. The nineteenth century witnessed the so-called triumph of the middle classes. Although there were still a few dukes and princes, the minor courts were fast disappearing, and the major ones no longer supported private orchestras. It was the upper middle class that now called the tune, founding publicly supported orchestras and building concert halls seating hundreds, or thousands, of people. Seventeen men may have sufficed to play Bach's *Brandenburg Concertos* in the music room at the court of Anhalt-Cöthen (particularly as the prince, for whom the concert was being given, was both player and audience); but in a bourgeois concert hall with fifteen hundred listeners, there had to be a proportionate increase in the size of the orchestra and the volume of sound it could produce.

Berlioz always insisted that the theaters of his day were too large for the standard orchestra. If the music proceeded from a point too far away from the listener, "we *hear* but do not vibrate. Now we *must vibrate* ourselves with the instruments and voices, and be made to vibrate by them in order to have true musical sensations." (One wonders whether he would have been delighted or horrified by the decibels that shake the walls of a modern discothèque.) On one occasion, when he was asked to organize a concert in the giant exhibition hall of the 1844 Paris Industrial Exhibition—an event that perfectly expressed the power of the burgeoning bourgeoisie—he filled the stage with a chorus and orchestra of 1,022 men and women, about evenly divided between singers and instrumentalists. It took six assistant conductors and chorus masters to control this vast socio-musical enterprise. But, as Berlioz declared, "... notwithstanding the acoustic defects of the place, I do not think that such an effect has often been produced." At one point, he himself was overcome by the sound. "I was seized with such a fit of nervous trembling that my teeth chattered as though I were in a violent fever ... the concert had to be stopped for some time."

Berlioz relates that the concert took in 32,000 francs, but that only 800 of them went into his pocket. That was typical of the pitiless economics that ultimately turned him against the bourgeois society of his day. "I belong to a nation that has ceased to be interested in the nobler manifestations of intelligence, and whose only deity is the golden calf," he wrote bitterly when he was fifty. "The industrialism of art, followed by all the base instincts it flatters and caresses, marches at the head of an absurd procession. ..." At the root of his difficulties lay a nineteenth-century dilemma that the twentieth has yet to resolve: since it is no longer the princes who support the artist, he must now look to the general public for a livelihood. But the public's taste is notoriously shallow and untrustworthy. It prefers commonplaces and will rarely trouble itself over complex or unfamiliar matters. This attitude is not calculated to decrease the artist's sense of estrangement from his audience.

The theme of the artist's alienation from society is hardly a nineteenth-century invention, of course, but it was with the romantics that the theme became almost an obsession. "My joys, my griefs, my passions and my powers,/ Made me a stranger," says Byron's hero Manfred, summing up the poet's own feeling of isolation from the world. Manfred is a mountain climber (Byron, with his lameness, could follow him only in his imagination). And he likes to stand poised on the edge of an alpine abyss, a typically romantic situation from which the artist-misanthrope can look down on a distant world. This is the romantic's favorite view of himself with respect to the rest of society. He takes risks but is rewarded with a vantage point like that of an eagle. High above conventional mankind, he is a solitary spectator whose figure is outlined against the sky.

The curious melancholia that accompanies this sense of unbridgeable remoteness between the artist and other people was known as *Le Spleen* among the French romantics. Berlioz describes it in his memoirs when he writes about his youthful emotions on May mornings in the meadows of his native Dauphiné:

> Silence ... the faint rustling of the wheat, stirred by the soft morning air ... the utter calm ... the dull throbbing of my own heart. ... Life was so far, far away from me. ... On the remote horizon the Alpine glaciers flashed like gems in the light of the morning sun ... below me, Meylan ... and beyond the Alps, Italy, Naples, Posilippo ... burning passions ... and unfathomable and secret joy. ... Oh for wings across the space! I want life and love and enthusiasm and burning kisses, I want more and fuller life!

No other musician succeeded so well as Berlioz in describing the great *Sehnsucht* ("yearning") that underlies the romantic imagination. And he was not only able to put it into words; he expressed it musically in many of his works, notably in the meadow scene of the *Symphonie fantastique*. Here his hero is in the country, thinking of his beloved as he listens to two shepherds in the distance playing a *ranz-des-vaches* (the tune used by Swiss shepherds to call their flocks). At the end of the movement, according to Berlioz' program note, "one of the shepherds resumes the melody, but the other answers him no more. ... Sunset ... distant rolling of thunder ... loneliness ... silence. ..."

Something of this anguished mood can be found in all of the great romantics, but its most voluptuous expression occurs in the music of Chopin—in the nocturnes, préludes, and ballades, whose "despairing beauty of sound" has never been approached by any other composer. Chopin's piano music is a world in itself, and unlike Berlioz' symphonic realm, requires no literary explanations. He always avoided giving descriptive titles to his pieces, and deeply resented other people trying to do it for him (although there was no stopping the ladies who gushed "Play me your *Second Sigh*" or "I love your *Bells*!"). On rare occasions even he would resort to words. Describing his E Minor Piano

Two Delacroix portraits (below) show Frédéric Chopin and his mistress George Sand. The pair met late in the decade of the 1830's and traveled to the Mediterranean where the young but already consumptive Chopin composed some of his Twenty-Four Preludes for the piano. Romance frequently overtook susceptible pianists of the period; the young woman at right, sculpted by Jean Pierre Dantan, reflects this indulgent mood.

Concerto to a distant friend, for example, he wrote that the second movement was intended to convey "the impression you get when your eye wanders over a moonlit landscape you know well and love much" —a description that would have done credit to Heine. His real concern, however, was for the musical effect he was creating. "Have I made it haunting?" he asked. "I wonder—time will tell."

Virtually everything important that Chopin wrote is for the piano. The orchestra simply did not interest him, and his songs are a minor part of his output. His contribution to music consists of more than two hundred piano works that are, for the most part, as brief and brilliant as was his own life. He gave these works elastic forms that could express his moods of the moment: the impromptu, the scherzo, the concert waltz, the polonaise, the mazurka. In the hands of the right pianist they can still sound today as though they had just been freshly improvised.

Yet, there is much more hard work and artifice in Chopin's works than meets the ear. "His creation was spontaneous and miraculous," writes George Sand, with whom he lived for ten years. "He found it without seeking it, without foreseeing it. It came on his piano suddenly, complete, sublime, or it sang in his head during a walk, and he was impatient to play it to himself." But then, she adds, began a period of agonizing struggle, while he had second thoughts about what he had

written. "He shut himself up in his room for whole days, weeping, walking, breaking his pen, repeating and altering a bar a hundred times, writing and effacing it as many times, and recommencing the next day with a minute and desperate perseverance. He spent six weeks over a single page to write it at last as he had noted it down at the very first."

Chopin worked with a range of chromatic harmonies that were like Delacroix' palette with its reds, yellows, and grays. Often the whole structure of a Chopin piece is determined by the contrasting "colors" of his harmony, as it moves from brighter to darker levels of sound. His style is so subtle and luminous that it sounds most at home in the intimate acoustics of a drawingroom. That, rather than any inability to play fortissimo, was why Chopin hated performing in large concert halls, and why he did so only rarely during his later years. His natural habitat was the aristocratic salon of a Prince Czartoryski or a Baron Rothschild, where he could play to a small, select circle of cultivated listeners. Berlioz recalled these occasions:

> What emotions he could then call forth! In what ardent and melancholy reveries he loved to pour out his soul! It was usually towards midnight that he gave himself up with greatest abandon, when the big butterflies of the salon had left ... then, obedient to the mute petition of some beautiful, intelligent eyes, he became a poet. ...

Everyone who knew Chopin agreed that he was "the most sensitive genius in existence," and it was often remarked that in some mysterious way he resembled his music the way some people resemble their dogs. "The particular sound he drew from the piano was like the glance of his eyes," noted Ernest Legouvé. "The slightly ailing delicacy of his fingers was allied to the poetic melancholy of his nocturnes, and the careful attention he conferred on sartorial details helped explain the worldly elegance of certain parts of his work."

What was less evident in Chopin's work was the energy and concentration that he brought to his task. A composer who dies of tuberculosis at thirty-nine and yet produces as many masterpieces as Chopin

With its changing friends and lovers, the life of the romantic artist was an art unto itself. Above, George Sand entertains her friends at a country romp: Franz Liszt kneeling, Delacroix standing, and Chopin poised as a parrot on the hostess's hand. In the realistic painting below, at right, Liszt plays the piano for his kneeling mistress, the Countess d' Agoult, who later wrote novels under the name Daniel Stern, and for his friends (from left) Alexandre Dumas, Berlioz, George Sand, Paganini, and Gioacchino Rossini.

did could hardly have been "dying all his life," as Berlioz suggested. He had to possess the kind of iron discipline usually attributed to men of action rather than poets and intellectuals. For that matter, his life should be written as a success story rather than a tragedy. A young man of humble origins takes foreign capitals by storm, becomes a world figure, dines with princes, but never loses the common touch. With his indulgent mistress, George Sand, he sometimes acted the spoiled child, but essentially he was rock hard and quite unspoilable. Robert Schumann sensed as much when he heard Chopin's music; here, he decided, were "cannon buried in flowers."

Franz Liszt is known to have envied Chopin's "vaporously fluid" way of playing the piano, which, he said, made the melody undulate to and fro, "like a skiff driven over the waves." During the early years of their friendship, Liszt learned to imitate Chopin's style so successfully that one evening, playing in a darkened room at George Sand's estate, he tricked their most intimate friends into believing that it was the poetic Chopin, not the fiery Liszt, who was improvising for them. Their friendship, however, was destined to end in a falling out. Liszt was far too much the extrovert, the man of the theater, and his incessant exuberance got on Chopin's nerves. Their temperamental differences, of course, were reflected in the sounds they produced at the piano. "Chopin carried you with him into a dreamland, in which you would have liked to dwell forever," wrote Sir Charles Hallé, who first heard them in 1836. "Liszt was all sunshine and dazzling splendor, subjugating his hearers with a power that none could withstand. For him there were no difficulties of execution, the most incredible seeming child's play under his fingers."

As a composer, Liszt was far more erratic and unpredictable than Chopin. Many of his early salon pieces and bravura studies were written simply as crowd pleasers. "I am the slave of the public," he used to say rather ruefully. But his greatest works, such as the *Sonetti del Petrarca* or the *Paganini Etudes*, are stamped with an irresistible power and breadth of vision. With his hands freely ranging the keyboard, destroying the classical division of labor between right-hand treble and left-hand bass, he was prepared to take all kinds of harmonic chances. During much of his career Liszt was really an avant-gardist disguised as a matinée idol.

Liszt lived nearly twice as long as Chopin, and his career spanned virtually the whole romantic epoch. As a child prodigy he had been kissed on the forehead by Beethoven, and he had published his first music in a collection together with Schubert. Later he befriended Felix Mendelssohn and Robert Schumann as well as Chopin and Berlioz; he helped Rossini to his last success and Wagner to his first; he taught and aided two whole generations of younger musicians, including Bedřich Smetana and Edward MacDowell. And finally, in his old age, he discovered and sponsored the young Russians of the Borodin-Moussorgsky circle. Emotionally as well as musically he was always ready to try something new. "You cannot expect from an artist that he should forego love in any form whatever," he once wrote to a woman who was trying to hold him back, "neither the sort that moves the senses and emotions, nor the ascetic and mystical forms of love."

In Paris, as a young man, he was no less famed for his affairs of the heart than for his piano technique—which was, of course, entirely to be expected from a romantic artist of such Mephistophelean charm. In 1835, when he was twenty-four, he eloped to Switzerland with the blonde, blue-eyed Countess Maria d'Agoult, a married woman of great social distinction who was described by a friend as "six inches of ice over twenty feet of lava." They spent the next few years in the Alps and in Italy, where Liszt composed the miniature tone poems and landscape sketches afterward published as *Années de Pelérinage* ("Years of Pilgrimage"). The countess saw herself as "a chosen one, destined as an offering for the salvation of this divine genius," and she bore him three children (one of whom, Cosima, was destined to become the second, and decisive, wife of Richard Wagner).

Their relationship, however, lasted no longer than did that of Chopin and Sand, or of Berlioz and Harriet Smithson. Soon, Liszt was on the road again. Traveling in a horse-drawn *Reisewagen* that served as a salon by day and a boudoir by night, he lived a vagabond life that took him to every capital in Europe from Portugal to Turkey. He was the pianist of the hour and of the century. The crosses and medals he had received from kings and princes jangled rhythmically on his chest when he played in court dress. In Budapest his countrymen acclaimed him a national hero (although he never learned to speak Hungarian; German and, preferably, French, were his usual languages).

Then, in his late thirties, Liszt settled down in the town of Weimar with the Princess Carolyn Sayn-Wittgenstein, the estranged wife of a Tsarist nobleman. Here, with an orchestra at his disposal for the first

Photographed (above) but never recorded by the phonograph that was invented six years before his death in 1886, the Hungarian piano virtuoso Franz Liszt was concerned that he had not written down all the great works he carried about in his imagination. Instead, he had expended his considerable energies at the keyboard, astonishing audiences and teaching others to play, or by taking time out for the turbulent love affairs that seemed not to cease even when he donned clerical garb (caricatured at right).

time, he followed Berlioz' example and composed a long series of tone poems for orchestra, including the great *Faust* and *Dante* symphonies, and the well-known *Les Préludes* (a work based on Alphonse de Lamartine's *Méditation*: "What is life but a series of preludes to that unknown song whose first solemn note is sounded by death?").

Meanwhile an era was drawing to a close. The brave romanticism of the 1830's gave way to the frustrations and disappointments of 1848, the year when a wave of abortive revolutions swept through Europe. Mendelssohn died in 1847; Chopin in 1849; and by 1854 Schumann was incurably ill in a mental asylum. At mid-century Berlioz could write, "If not at the end of my career, I am at any rate on the last steep decline. . . ." In music as well as literature and politics, Europe was settling down to the red-plush respectability that, in England at least, became known as the Victorian Era. Yet Liszt continued to have adventures of the old school and to write music that was harmonically more audacious than ever, as though the Philistines simply did not exist.

He moved to Rome in the 1860's and took minor orders in the Catholic Church to become, at least nominally, the "Abbé" Liszt. He was not a priest, however, and (fortunately, as it turned out) did not have to take a vow of celibacy. Nor did his cassock detract in any way from his charm; "women still go perfectly crazy over him," a friend observed. One of his piano pupils in Rome, the "Cossack Countess," Olga Janina, fell in love with him and resolved, "he shall be mine or I will kill him." As she afterward told the story, he surrendered to her without much of a struggle. But the next morning, as Liszt slept, it occurred to this wild Ukrainian horsewoman that he might have regrets, that thoughts of remorse would take him from her. Armed with a poisoned dagger, she braced herself for the awakening. "One tiny puncture and he was mine for all eternity, for we would lie under the same winding sheet in the same tomb. I held the dagger in the hollow of my hand and waited for his first word. It was one of love. He was saved."

If Liszt realized how narrow had been his escape, he must have breathed a sigh of relief not only for himself but for art's sake, for by then he was the last of the great romantics. And the music that he wrote during the years before his death in 1886 was curiously dissonant and experimental, preparing the way for modernists like Claude Debussy and Béla Bartók, who were to consider him one of their most important influences. Among his own students there were none who understood the "bizarre" pieces of the seventy-year-old Liszt. "Is one allowed to write such a thing?" one of them asked about the dissonant *Csárdás Macabre*. "Is one allowed to listen to it?" But Liszt himself had lost nothing of his romantic sense of distance and detachment from an alien world. His motto had become *"Wir können warten"* ("We can wait"). "I have to accustom myself to treating my music with a sort of systematic disregard and passive resignation," he told a friend. "The fact is that 'Monsieur Litz' is welcome everywhere when he shows himself at the piano. . . . But they will not let him think and compose his own way. . . . They may be right, but . . . I am filled with the spirit of resistance and determined to follow my own path to the end without pampering or deceiving myself."

7

In Search of Musical Alternatives

DOCTOR ALEXANDER BORODIN, professor of organic chemistry at the St. Petersburg Academy of Medicine, paid a visit to the aging Abbé Liszt in Jena during the summer of 1877 and, to his delighted surprise, was welcomed with open arms. Liszt, it seemed, already knew all about the music that Borodin had been composing in his spare time; he even knew the doctor's First Symphony by heart. "Your first movement is perfect," Liszt told him as soon as the introductions were out of the way. "Your *andante* is a masterpiece. The *scherzo* is enchanting ... and then, *this* passage is so ingenious!"—and his long fingers picked out a skittish progression of distant intervals that, in the symphony, are played by pizzicato strings.

Speaking in an excited mixture of French and German, he confided to Borodin (who, in turn, recorded their conversation in a long letter to his wife) how much he admired Russian music, as opposed to the local product. "You know Germany," he said. "It is full of composers. I am lost in a sea of music that threatens to entirely submerge me; but Heavens, how insipid it all is, not one living idea! With you there exists a vitalizing stream."

This was a curious compliment, coming from a composer who was considered one of the founders of the *Neudeutsche* ("New German") movement, and the father-in-law of Richard Wagner at that. But as if to prove that this was not just a momentary lapse, Liszt carried on in this fashion for the next three weeks, until it was time for his guest to make his departure. And when Borodin returned for another visit four years later, Liszt had still more flattering things to tell him. "You Russians are indispensable to us," he insisted. "You have a quick and vital spring; the future belongs to you, while here I see nothing but lifeless stagnation all about."

In search of a native Russian idiom, Nikolai Rimsky-Korsakov looked to the folk songs and tales he had absorbed during a country childhood. Costume sketches for his satirical opera La Coq d'Or *(left, by Alexander Benois) reveal the Oriental flavor so often found in the composer's work.*

There was something almost heretical in Liszt's assessment of the musical situation. In the 1870's and 1880's it was generally taken for granted that Wagner held a patent on "the music of the future," and indeed the great Wagner festival at Bayreuth was a living monument to that idea. But Liszt, with his extraordinary perception of new values in music, was well aware that romanticism (even *post*romanticism) had run out of steam, and that serious music was now badly in need of rejuvenation. The "lifeless stagnation all about" (and Bayreuth was less than a hundred miles away) was caused primarily by the rhythmic inertia of the German symphonic tradition, whose basic rhythms tended to fall either into the ONE-two-three-four pattern of the march, or the SLIDE-two-three of the waltz, invariably punctuated with the thumping of a big bass drum. Now at last a fresh wind was blowing from the east, where the Russian composers were able to draw on sources of inspiration hitherto untapped by serious musicians—peasant songs, folkdances, the sound of shepherds' pipes and balalaikas, and the strange, haunting harmonies of the choruses that serfs sang as they worked in the fields.

This search for musical alternatives had begun with Mikhail Glinka, a gentleman composer from St. Petersburg who had learned much of what he knew about music from his uncle's orchestra—an orchestra of serfs, of which his uncle owned the players as well as the instruments. In

The music of Russian peasants was written down by gentlemen: Mikhail Glinka (below) was one of the first to use peasant tunes in operas created for the ears of the aristocracy; and it was for aristocratic eyes that P. Malyavin painted three peasants in song (left). The prerevolutionary Russian spirit was evoked in the music of an informal but pivotal group called The Mighty Five and in such views as that opposite, which illustrates a popular song concerning a troika passing through a Russian landscape.

1830 Glinka had gone to Italy and learned to imitate Vincenzo Bellini, a composer who dominated the Italian operatic scene. He was successful enough to have had some music published in Milan, but it suddenly dawned on him that he ought to be composing like a Russian instead. To accomplish this ambition he had only instinct to guide him. The term "folksong" had not yet been invented, nor the whole folklore mystique that went with it. But Glinka knew and loved the "doleful Russian songs" he had heard among the peasants, and he proceeded to incorporate such tunes into the score of his patriotic opera *A Life for the Tsar.*

When the opera was first performed in 1836, his music struck the aristocrats of St. Petersburg like a slap in the face. Countess Nesselrode, wife of the foreign minister, said it was disgraceful to put onstage the songs she heard from her serfs. It was coachmen's music—"*C'est la musique des cochers!*" Her remark made the rounds of the salons; Glinka muttered that a coachman is a more sensible person than a gentleman. In any case, the Tsar himself was moved to tears by the opera,

and it was generally agreed that Glinka had succeeded in launching a Russian national school.

It remained for a group of composers in the next generation, however, to bring his ideas to fruition. The so-called *Moguchaya Koochka* —literally "the mighty handful," but better known in English as The Mighty Five—were easily the most astonishing collection of dilettantes and geniuses ever assembled into a school of composition. There was Borodin, the illegitimate son of a Georgian prince, a chemistry professor as well as a composer; César Cui, a military engineer (later a lieutenant general) and composer; Nikolai Rimsky-Korsakov, the naval cadet turned composer and inspector of naval bands; Modeste Moussorgsky, the Imperial Guard officer turned composer; and Mili Balakirev, the only one to begin as a professional musician, although he sacrificed a promising career as a concert pianist to devote his life to the cause of a new Russian music. It was he who had brought the *Koochka* together and, as Rimsky-Korsakov wrote, "he held us absolutely spellbound by his talents, his authority, his magnetism."

Borodin was the first of the five to gain recognition in Western Europe, and then it was for his research into the properties of aldehydes as well as for his symphonies and the tone poem *In the Steppes of Central Asia*. "Borodin was an extremely cordial and cultured man, pleasant and witty to talk with," writes Rimsky-Korsakov in his memoirs. And he goes on to describe Borodin's working habits:

On visiting him I often found him working in the laboratory which adjoined his apartment. When he sat over his retorts filled with some colorless gas and distilled it by means of a tube from one vessel into another—I used to tell him that he was "transfusing emptiness into vacancy." Having finished his work, he would go with me to his apartment, where we began musical operations or conversations, in the midst of which he used to jump up, run back to the laboratory to see whether something had not burned out or boiled over; meanwhile he filled the corridor with incredible sequences from successions of ninths or sevenths.

In the end it was the chemistry that got the lion's share of Borodin's divided attention, since he rarely had time to write music, as he said, "except during my summer holiday, or when some ailment compels me to keep to my rooms." Both his magnum opus, the opera *Prince Igor*, and his Third Symphony were left unfinished at his death in 1887.

Moussorgsky, the mightiest of the five in terms of talent, had a constitutional reluctance to finish anything. "I think, think, think, think of many sensible things," he conceded, "and many plans swirl through my head; if one would only bring these to fulfillment it would be splendid." When he resigned his commission in the exclusive Preobrazhensky Guards regiment in order to do great things for Russian music, his friends were exceedingly doubtful. Vladimir Stassov, the *Koochka*'s literary mentor, called him "a perfect idiot." To Balakirev he seemed little better—"practically an idiot." Even Borodin, who was willing enough to be impressed by Moussorgsky's work (what there was of it), had to admit that "I was incredulous when he told me he intended to devote himself to serious music."

A turning point came in 1861, however, when Tsar Alexander II issued the proclamation emancipating the serfs, an edict that swept away the feudal system in Russia. The immediate effect of the edict on Moussorgsky was to send him to the provinces to straighten out his family's financial affairs. Living in the country during the summer months, he watched and listened carefully while working with the liberated peasants. "I have been raking hay, cooking jam and putting up pickles. . . . I am observing characteristic peasant women and typical peasant men—they may all come in handy. With how many fresh sides, untouched by art, the Russian nature swarms, oh, how many! and with what juicy ones, splendid ones. . . . A small part of that, which life has given to me, I have pictured in musical images. . . ."

He was collecting material and gathering strength for a creative breakthrough. "My music must be an artistic reproduction of human speech in all its finest shades, that is, the sounds of human speech, as the external manifestations of thought and feeling, must, without exaggeration or violence, become true, accurate music. . . ." This principle was applied to his opera *Boris Godunov* (with its extraordinary arias of speech heightened into song—the pleading beggar, the drunken vagabond, the storytelling priest, the exulting Tsar) as well as to a series of songs for solo voice and piano. These songs represent a milestone in the history of music: the *Sunless* cycle, the *Songs and Dances of Death*, and the astonishing cycle *The Nursery*, with texts by Moussorgsky himself illustrating episodes from child life.

A friend who was present when Liszt received a copy of *The Nursery* in 1873 and first tried it out on the piano relates that the experience was nothing short of a revelation. Liszt instantly understood what

Chemistry professor Alexander Borodin (left, above) composed his short list of twenty-one works whenever vacations or an illness gave him the leisure; his unfinished melodic opera Prince Igor *(première program at left) had to be shaped by Rimsky-Korsakov after Borodin fell dead at a masked ball. Borodin and Modeste Moussorgsky (above) were both in their twenties when* The Mighty Five *was formed in 1862; Moussorgsky's unfinished opera* Khovanshchina *(costume sketches for it are shown at right) was not performed until five years after his death.*

Overleaf: A *scene from Moussorgsky's opera* Boris Godunov *sets the stage for its protagonist, the Russian people, as represented by the opera's chorus.*

Moussorgsky was driving at. In the first song, the time indication changes with each bar, beginning with 7/4, continuing in 6/4 and 5/4, and reaching 3/2, 3/4, and 4/4—seventeen times within twenty-four measures. Yet, Liszt played it from the page with a power of expression that took his listeners' breath away. "Hardly had Liszt played, with great simplicity, several bars of this little song which clearly overcame him, than we were swept up in his emotion. . . . You should have heard Liszt crying out at each new page: 'How interesting! . . . and how new! . . . What discoveries! . . . No one else would have said it this way. . . .' And thousands of other exclamations of satisfaction and pleasure. . . ."

Liszt usually had a kind word for young composers with new ideas, but he was not easily carried away like this. Moussorgsky's songs excited him because they pointed the way out of the rhythmic and harmonic impasse of Western music. Their variable time-scheme was the much-needed antidote to the "lifeless stagnation all about."

At first there was a great deal of resistance to this kind of music, and not only from the Establishment. In his pursuit of peasant music, Moussorgsky had gone much further toward dissonance and "barbarity" than the others of the *Koochka*. And the more conservative Russian composers, notably Peter Ilich Tchaikovsky, dismissed him simply as a talented eccentric. "He has been too easily led away by the absurd theories of his set," Tchaikovsky wrote to his patroness, Madame von Meck. "He likes what is coarse, unpolished and ugly . . . and even seems proud of his want of skill, writing just as it comes to him, believing blindly in the infallibility of his genius. As a matter of fact his very original talent flashes forth now and again."

Tchaikovsky himself occupied the middle ground in the conflict between the so-called coachmen's music and the German orchestral tradition. On the whole, he regarded the *Koochka* as a group of presumptuous amateurs. "Their mockery of the schools and the classical masters, denial of authority and of the masterpieces, was nothing but ignorance. . . ." They, in turn, accused him of being too receptive to German and Italian influences instead of relying on Russian sources of inspiration.

Yet Tchaikovsky was nothing if not a truly Slavic composer. Although his symphonies and concertos conform more or less to classical German models, his style is always instantly recognizable as Russian. Indeed, his works often quote or adapt folksongs he had heard in the country: for example, the "blind beggar" tune that appears as the main theme of the first movement of the Piano Concerto No. 1 ("It is curious," he wrote, "that in Russia every blind beggar sings exactly the same tune with the same refrain"), the Polish folksong in the first movement of the Fifth Symphony, or the Ukrainian folk tune known as "The Crane," in the finale of the Second Symphony. Even the famous *andante cantabile* of the D Major String Quartet (which reduced Tolstoy to tears and is now known to popular music as "When It Is June on the Isle of May") began life as a beautiful Russian folksong that runs, "Vanya sat drinking; as he drank he thought of his sweetheart. . . ."

Even these relatively gentle (and not at all barbaric) translations of Slavic folksongs into a more international idiom were capable of rousing the guardians of the German tradition to outbursts of angry invective. Sensing that their musical hegemony was being threatened, they reacted by doing their best to discredit the challengers. When Tchaikovsky's utterly lyrical Violin Concerto was given its première in Vienna, for example, the critic Eduard Hanslick talked about the "savagery" of the first movement and railed against the finale. "It puts us in the midst of the brutal and wretched jollity of a Russian kermess. We see wild and vulgar faces, we hear curses, we smell bad brandy. . . . Tchaikovsky's Violin Concerto brings to us for the first time the horrid idea that there may be music that stinks in the ear."

Hanslick's review was written in 1881, by which time the world of serious music had split into three competing and mutually hostile camps: the nationalists on the periphery, and the feuding Wagnerians and Brahmsians at the center. The nationalists included not only the Russians but also the Czechs Bedřich Smetana and Antonín Dvořák, as well as the Norwegian Edvard Grieg—soon to be followed by Jean Sibelius in Finland and by three great Spanish composers, Isaac Albéniz, Enrique Granados, and Manuel de Falla.

In one way or another, each of these men drew on the folk traditions of his native country in order to assert his independence from classical models. "It is possible to say after a few bars: that is Mozart—that is Chopin," Smetana once explained to a friend. "If only one day it were possible to say after a few bars: that is Smetana. . . ." Although he established Prague as a Pan-Slavic musical center to rival Moscow and St. Petersburg, Smetana's brilliant career was cut short by deafness just as he reached the height of his powers. "If martyrs are still born today,

then I am the unhappiest of all," he wrote in 1883, "for fate has sentenced me to a silent tomb where the sound of human voices is unknown; I have never heard the greater part of my poetic creations [including the great cycle of tone poems *My Country*], but I have seen many times how the majority in the audience wept as they listened to the fruits of my mind!"

The Wagnerians, centered on their festival of music-drama at Bayreuth (they never called it opera), constituted a party unto themselves. By 1880 Wagner's "music of the future" had become almost a religious cult. Indeed, at one point Catholic newspapers warned that Wagner was trying to usurp the function of the Church by substituting his theater for the Mass. His influence, moreover, was symphonic as well as operatic, since the younger symphonists were profoundly affected by his orchestral style—the continual ebb and flow of chromatic harmonies, moving through carefully planned progressions of keys; the massive, glittering sound of his orchestra, with its leitmotiv themes serving as identity tags; and the brilliant use of sonic analogies drawn from nature. This was the sort of thing that George Bernard Shaw once catalogued as "music of river and rainbow, fire and forest ... the love music, the hammer and anvil music, the clumping of the giants, the tune of the young woodsman's horn . . . the dragon music and nightmare music and thunder and lightning music."

Wagner was an ultranationalist in his own right, preaching a murky gospel of Teutonism and salvation-by-music-drama. "I am the most German of beings," he wrote to his royal patron, Ludwig II of Bavaria. "I am the German spirit. Consult the incomparable magic of my works;

hold them side by side with everything else; you have no choice but to say—this is German." Despite his phobia of the French, Wagner had nearly as many French admirers as German, and every Bayreuth festival included a large delegation of musicians from Paris who had come to "join the faithful." Two generations of French poets, from Baudelaire to Mallarmé, Valéry, and Claudel, worshiped Wagner as the symbolist par excellence. Baudelaire confessed that on hearing Wagner he had the sensation of "letting myself be penetrated and invaded—a really sensual delight that resembles rising on the air or tossing upon the sea. . . ." And Emanuel Chabrier, one of the most vivacious of French composers, burst into tears at the thrill of hearing, at long last, the Prelude to *Tristan und Isolde* at Bayreuth. "Ten years," he sobbed into the ear of his neighbor, the composer Vincent d'Indy, "ten years I've been waiting for that A on the cellos!"

Johannes Brahms, living in Vienna, represented a more sober, less theatrical side of the German tradition. He never wrote an opera, had very little to do with program music, and did his best work within the

framework of forms developed by Mozart, Haydn, and Beethoven. But if the form is studiously classical, the content is glowing romantic. "One sees what can still be done with the old forms when someone comes along who knows how to handle them," remarked no less an authority than Wagner himself when the young Brahms came for a visit in 1864 and performed some of his piano music. But this adherence to old precedents ultimately proved to be more than Wagner and the futurists could bear. Even Tchaikovsky, who took a dim view of the Wagnerians, felt that Brahms' position was hopelessly outdated. "Isn't Brahms in reality a caricature of Beethoven?" he wrote to Madame von Meck. "Isn't this pretension to profundity and power detestable, because the contents that are poured into the Beethoven mould are not really of any value?"

At close range it was difficult to see that Brahms' conservatism concealed a radicalism of his own. He worked instinctively within the established order because the tightest forms provided the richest harmonic contrasts. Brahms was interested in sounding new depths, where Wagner's ambition was to reach new heights. One of Brahms' youthful notebooks contains a significant reference to the "inner sound" of music, and a reminder that "the real musician should reverberate with music within himself." This inward resonance was to become one of the hallmarks of Brahms' style, and involved the use of a rich, somber palette of instrumental colors in the middle range. Cello, French horn, and clarinet are cornerstones of his orchestral sound as well as of his chamber music. And in his vocal works, too, he often gravitates to the "serious" sound of low voices and dark chest tones.

Working within the classical tradition did not mean that he could avoid having to take musical risks. On the contrary, as Brahms pointed out, "you have no idea how it feels to hear behind you the tramp of a giant like Beethoven." And there were lessons for even the most revolutionary modernist in his four symphonies, his concertos, his vast output of chamber music, songs, and piano works. The twentieth-century innovator Arnold Schoenberg once said that Brahms' music had taught him four vital elements of style. The first was melodic asymmetry, "especially uneven numbers of measures; extension and contradiction of phrases." The second was elasticity of form, "not being stingy or cramped when clarity demands more space; carrying out each figure to the end." The third was "the systematic construction of movements," and the last was "economy, yet richness." There was, after all, much to be done with the old forms when someone came along who knew how to handle them.

8

Fin de Siècle

IN 1889 PARIS CELEBRATED the hundredth anniversary of the French Revolution by holding a great "universal exhibition" in the very heart of the city, on the Esplanade des Invalides and the Champ de Mars. No effort and expense was spared to make this the most spectacular world's fair of the century. The Eiffel Tower had been erected especially for the occasion. At 984 feet it was then the tallest structure in the world and one of the wonders of modern technology (although many leading artists and intellectuals had signed a petition against it, protesting that it would eclipse the rest of the city's monuments).

Besides the more conventional displays of commerce and industry, the exhibition provided a lavish sampling of exotic cultures from Africa and the Far East. There was a Buddhist temple, a Moroccan bazaar, a Chinese pavilion, a Senegalese village, a whole Cairo street in replica, a settlement of Congolese ivory carvers, a Vietnamese theatrical troupe, a village of Tonkinese silk weavers. For the composers who came to see them, some of these special exhibits opened the door to an utterly fascinating world of sounds they had never heard before, or had even been able to imagine, for this was, after all, long before the age of the all-hearing phonograph. Rimsky-Korsakov, for example, who came from Russia to conduct a pair of *Koochka* concerts at the Trocadéro, was intrigued by the warbling of the primitive Balkan Panpipes and by the music of the North African section. "At the Algerian café, in the dance of a little girl with a dagger, I was captivated by the sudden blows struck by a Negro on the large drum at the dancer's approach"—an effect he promptly appropriated, along with the Panpipes, for his next opera, *Mlada*.

In another part of the exhibition, the twenty-seven-year-old Claude Debussy made a discovery that was to have a decisive and lasting effect on his musical thinking. A gamelan orchestra from Java was encamped in the Dutch colonial section on the Esplanade des Invalides, and he spent many fruitful hours there listening to that astonishing barrage of rhythms and timbres, so totally unlike anything to be heard in a Western concert hall. The official review of the exhibition reported on this ensemble:

> The whole gamelan orchestra plays at once. There is the gamelan itself, a sort of "piano" of thin wooden slabs, played with wooden mallets. Then the *bonang*, a set of bronze gongs shaped like pots and arranged

on a table, played with padded sticks; it produced two scales of full-bodied sounds. Then the *rebab*, a two-string violin; the *selumpret*, a sort of oboe; and finally the *tam-tam*. It's like living in a dream. Imagine a melody from another world, elusive and thrilling, the fluid rhythms constantly moving within a sort of ritual monotony, translated into the sonority of muffled bells, muted strings, delicate woodblocks, attenuated gongs and cymbals. . . . Yes, we are truly in Indra's paradise!

Debussy never forgot this first encounter with the music of the Orient. The Javanese gamelan, he wrote to his friend Pierre Louÿs, was able "to express every shade of meaning, even those that cannot be described in words, and which make our tonic and dominant seem like phantoms meant to impress small naughty children." And in an article written many years later, he maintained that all music should be like the Javanese: "Their conservatory is the eternal rhythm of the sea, the wind in the leaves, and the thousand little natural sounds which they understand very well without having to consult some arbitrary treatise. . . . And if one would listen without European prejudice to the charm of their percussion, one would have to admit that ours is nothing but the barbarous noise of a traveling circus."

With the sound of the gamelan still fresh in his memory, he composed the piano piece *Pagodes*, with its tinkling bell effects and Oriental scales. But it was not just a matter of borrowing a few picturesque devices. The experience of the gamelan reinforced Debussy's preoccupation with instrumental textures and supplied the basis for that shimmering *pointillisme* of sound that was to become known, much against his wishes, as impressionism. The sound of his orchestra in works like the symphonic sketches *La Mer* ("The Sea") and the two nocturnes *Nuages* ("Clouds") and *Fêtes* ("Festivals") has been described as a "stylized gamelan." It was no accident that when Debussy's String Quartet was first performed, one of the critics complained that it sounded too much like the Javanese music at the exhibition, with "bounding rhythms, violent harmonic jerks, alternating with languid melodies and pizzicato effects suggestive of guitars and mandolins."

One of the elements that attracted Debussy to Oriental music was its spontaneity; he wanted his own music to sound as though it had "not been written down." At the same time, it suggested a viable alternative to the rhythmic clichés of postromantic music. Above all, the pentatonic scales of the East influenced the coloring of his harmonies, just as Chinese painting and Japanese prints influenced the art nouveau of Paris—the veiled dancers of Toulouse-Lautrec and the fashion-plate figures of Pierre Bonnard. Debussy's art is essentially one of elusive harmonies that refuse to remain within a key, but rise and fall like the tides. He will revert to the Middle Ages for some of his effects, or to ancient Greek modes as well as pentatonic scales, using a succession of dissonances and unrelated chords that are rarely resolved in accordance with the precepts of traditional harmony.

Debussy had loved the forbidden fruits of harmony even before his Oriental enlightenment. One of his fellow students at the Paris Conservatoire, Maurice Emmanuel, remembered how Debussy's earliest improvisations used to annoy the faculty but fascinate his classmates:

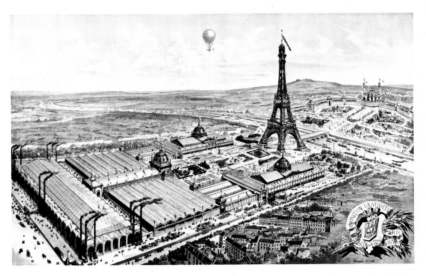

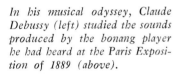

In his musical odyssey, Claude Debussy (left) studied the sounds produced by the bonang player he had heard at the Paris Exposition of 1889 (above).

Overleaf: *Leon Bakst created an enchanted forest in his scenic sketch for Maurice Ravel's* Daphnis et Chloé. *Commissioned by Sergei Diaghilev of the Ballet Russe, the ballet was first performed in 1912.*

At the piano we heard chromatic groanings in imitation of the buses going down the Faubourg Poissonnière, groups of consecutive fifths and octaves, sevenths which instead of being resolved in the proper way actually led to the note above or were not resolved at all; shameful "false relations"; chords of the ninth on all degrees of the scale; chords of the eleventh and thirteenth; all the notes of the diatonic scale heard at once in fantastic arrangements; shimmering sequences of arpeggios contrasted with trills played by both hands on three notes simultaneously. For more than an hour he held us spellbound around the piano, his shock of tousled hair shaking as he played.

This, in effect, was the whole of Debussy's harmonic arsenal. Although his idiom became more refined with the years, its basic vocabulary never changed. He seemed always to have the knack of combining, as one of the titles of his préludes has it, *Les sons et les parfums*—both the sounds and the perfumes of a poetic metaphor. He became a master at creating brilliantly evocative pictures out of "atmospheric vibrations": the *Soirée dans grenade* (although he had never seen Granada), the *Cloches à travers les feuilles* ("Bells Heard Through the Leaves"), or *La Cathédrale engloutie* ("The Engulfed Cathedral").

Debussy brought the nineteenth century to a close and inaugurated the modern harmonic revolution in France, although not without help from another musical impressionist who had fallen under the gamelan's spell in 1889. Maurice Ravel was only fourteen at the time, and still a student at the Conservatoire, yet he too, in later years, was to base some of his finest works on the Oriental scales to which he was introduced at the Paris exhibition.

Where Debussy had discovered the inspiration for *Pagodes*, Ravel found the material for his portrait of an *Impératrice des pagodes* and the hilarious duet between the Teapot and the Chinese Cup in *L'Enfant et les sortilèges* ("The Child and the Sorcerers"). Ravel, being thirteen years younger than Debussy and a great admirer of his music, could hardly avoid following in his footsteps. Debussy wrote the *Children's Corner* suite, Ravel the *Mother Goose*; Debussy an *Ibéria*, Ravel a *Rapsodie espagnole*; Debussy *Le jet d'eau*, Ravel the *Jeux d'eau* (both depict fountains). Both composers wrote some of their finest songs to

119

fin de siècle poems by Verlaine and Mallarmé. Ravel's *Miroirs* and the first series of Debussy's *Images*, both published in 1905, are virtually mirror images of each other. Chronologically it was not always Ravel who followed Debussy: the *Ondine* of Ravel's *Gaspard de la nuit* for piano is dated 1908, five years before the *Ondine* of Debussy's second book of préludes for piano.

In any case, the affinities are deceptive; temperamentally, Debussy and Ravel were worlds apart. The pianist Ricardo Viñes once summed up their metabolic differences by saying that the "magnificently ugly" Debussy reminded him of "some conspicuous condottiere or an honorable Calabrian bandit," while the slender, elegant Ravel resembled "a former jockey, profitably retired from the turf." Relations between them were actually quite cordial until their disciples started feuding—"too many stupid meddlers seemed to take pleasure in making a misunderstanding inevitable," a friend noted; then the two composers stopped visiting each other. Yet their respect for each other remained reciprocal, and both regretted the break.

Ravel sounds most like Debussy in the *Shéhérazade* song cycle of 1903—three "Persian" poems set to music while he was still under the spell of Debussy's great opera *Pelléas et Mélisande*. From that point on, however, Ravel developed a style of his own, which is far more linear and hard edged, maintaining a sense of classical detachment that the critics persisted in calling "cold blooded" and artificial. For the rest of his career, Ravel was invariably depicted as "the Swiss watchmaker" who could fabricate works of seventeen-jewel precision but was lacking in "depths of feeling." Understandably, Ravel got very tired of this approach. "Hasn't it ever occurred to these people," he asked irritably, "that I might be artificial by nature?"

If Debussy's point of departure was often the "sonorous halo" of a particular image, Ravel's was usually a rhythmic action of some sort—a strutting peacock or a slinking cat, the physical movement of a dancer (*Boléro* and *La Valse*), or even the ticking of clocks (*L'Heure espagnole*). He was probably the first composer to admire the "bizarre and magnificent" atmosphere of a factory, "and the wonderful symphony of moving belts, whistles and terrific hammer-blows in which you become submerged. . . . How much music there is in all this!"

When the ballet impresario Sergei Diaghilev came to Paris in 1909, he commissioned both Debussy and Ravel to write music for his Ballet Russe. Debussy composed one of his most dazzling, restless scores, *Jeux*, about two girls and a man pretending to look for a lost tennis ball. Ravel wrote a ballet based on the legend of Daphnis and Chloë. His starting point, in this case, was a spectacular ballet movement that had caught his eye at an earlier Diaghilev production. "I remember," writes his friend M. D. Calvocoressi, "that the very first bars that Ravel wrote were inspired by the memory of a wonderful leap sideways which Nijinsky (who was to be Daphnis) used to perform in a *pas seul* in *Le Pavillon d'Armide*, a ballet produced by Diaghilev that very season; and that they were intended to provide the opportunity for similar leaps—the pattern characterized by a run and a long pause, which runs through Daphnis's dances. . . ."

Debussy's 1902 opera Pelléas et Mélisande *(program cover, above) was much admired by the impeccable Ravel (left) with whom Debussy, the more subjective composer, is often compared. Both men wrote music for the symbolist poets of their day, and both wrote ballets for Diaghilev that were danced by Nijinsky, shown in Valentine Gross's 1913 drawing at right with two ballerinas in Debussy's* Jeux.

In a curiously graphic way, this famous *volte-face* of Nijinsky's symbolizes Ravel's whole relationship to the rest of the musical world of the early twentieth century. At the time he was writing some of his best-known works, several leading contemporaries—notably Arnold Schoenberg, Igor Stravinsky, and Béla Bartók—were beginning to make the great leap forward into unrestricted dissonance and atonality. Others, like Giacomo Puccini and Richard Strauss, preferred to stay rooted to the spot where traditional harmony prevailed. Ravel, after taking a running start as an *enfant terrible* of French music, executed a deft flanking maneuver that landed him off to one side, about midway between the avant-garde and the conservatives. In the years following *Daphnis et Chloé*, the modernist procession gradually passed him by. World War I, in the last year of which Debussy died of cancer, interrupted Ravel's career. When he returned from volunteer service as an ambulance driver, he still had twenty years of work ahead of him, yet he now belonged among the Old Masters rather than the Young Turks. Although he could write "problem music" as difficult as the next man's, he neither ventured beyond the limits of tonal harmony nor into the deeper waters of theoretical speculation. "Music does not need philosophy," he told the Viennese critic Paul Stefan.

But that was decidedly a French view of the matter. In Beethoven country—Vienna, Munich, Berlin—composers were accustomed to spending a good deal of time philosophizing about their art. Tradition demanded a certain amount of profundity from the serious musician, and after Wagner had established himself as a composer-intellectual of sorts, the whole German musical establishment took on an increasingly philosophical air. Sometimes, of course, the metaphysics resided chiefly in the program notes—as in Richard Strauss's *Also sprach Zarathustra*, whose Nietzschean subject serves as hardly more than a pretext for some particularly sensuous musicmaking. Characteristically, when the music revolution finally came to Vienna and Berlin, it was not just a change of styles but a whole elaborate methodology: the Schoenberg theory, supported by a school, a textbook, a manifesto, and a number of attendant interpreters.

Strauss, the leading German composer of the turn of the century, encountered most of the same problems as Debussy, especially the question of diminishing harmonic and rhythmic returns. His solutions, however, tended to be more conventional and Wagnerian. He owed his meteoric rise to fame as the "golden youth" of the 1890's to a series of richly orchestrated, excitingly illustrated tone poems, each of which represents a triumph not only of inspiration but of mechanics, acoustics, and logistics. His *Alpine Symphony*, to take an extreme example, calls for the collective and synchronous operation of at least eighteen first and sixteen second violins, twelve violas, ten cellos, eight basses, two piccolos, four flutes, three oboes, an English horn, a heckelphone, two clarinets in A-flat, two clarinets in B-flat, two clarinets in C, three bassoons, a contra bassoon, four horns, four trumpets, four trombones, four tenor tubas, two bass tubas, two harps, an organ, a wind machine, a thunder machine, a glockenspiel, cymbals, bass and side drums, a triangle, a tam-tam, a celesta, two sets of timpani, and "in the distance," a satellite band of twelve horns, two trumpets, and two trombones.

Any man capable of mobilizing and controlling so vast an apparatus for satisfying the human need for musical expression fulfilled a highly respected function in the bourgeois society of the *fin de siècle*. Nineteenth-century Germany was the one nation in the world that supported a dozen institutions of this kind, under conductors like Karl Muck, Arthur Nikisch, and Felix Weingartner. It was Strauss, doubling as composer and conductor, who devised the most successful new programs and applications for these superb musical facilities. He did not invent the tone poem any more than D. W. Griffith invented the movies, but like the latter he expanded the form to make it more meaningful and intriguing.

Both Strauss and Griffith were dream merchants of a sort, marshaling complex technical resources to stimulate and inspire audiences; to shock, soothe, uplift, and titillate. Debussy already said of Strauss's music: "It's just like cinematography." His tone poem *Till Eulenspiegel's Merry Pranks*, produced in 1895, is a typical case in point. Strauss stressed its "old-time, roguish" antecedents and its classical rondo form. But it is basically a new kind of music—an eighteen-minute comedy

Richard Strauss (above) chose to follow Wagner in developing the dramatic function of music, although he introduced modern harmonies to his works. Strauss's works, especially the lighter operas, were much loved, and in 1910 his native Munich treated him to a Strauss week, as announced in the poster at right.

with a spectacular cast, including eight horns, six trumpets, and a bass tuba. The twenty-four subtitles suggested by the composer might have been written for a silent-film version of the same scenario: "Off for new pranks," "Just wait, you hypocrites!" "She really has made an impression on him," "A kind refusal is still a refusal," and so on. In the final scene, when the prankster has been marched off to the gallows, a seemingly breathless flute trill is said to depict "the filtering out of the last air from the man dangling at the rope."

From the late 1880's until World War I, Strauss's tone poems drew the same sort of audience, and were discussed with the same avid interest, as today's art films. Newspaper critics engaged in earnest debates over the psychology of *Don Juan*, the imagery of *Don Quixote*, the ethics of *Zarathustra* (eighty years after it was written, *Zarathustra* became the theme music for Stanley Kubrick's film *2001: A Space Odyssey*). In *Death and Transfiguration*, Strauss anticipated the modern medical drama: "the sick man on his bed" undergoes a "pain motif," "fever motif," "groaning motif," "life-preservation motif," until the "last stroke of Death's ironhammer" brings "deliverance . . . transfiguration of the world." In his *Synfonia domestica* of 1904, a baby gurgles in

The elegant interior at left is a scenic sketch for Der Rosenkavalier, *a popular Strauss opera in which the composer's bold orchestral color manifests itself. At right a seductive Salome, painted by Gustav Klimt, evokes the heroine of Oscar Wilde's verse play, the play on which Strauss based his 1905 opera* Salome.

its bath, a glockenspiel chimes the hours, and a husband-and-wife argument is disguised as a double fugue.

Not long afterward, however, Strauss conceded that he no longer took pleasure in writing symphonies. The *Alpine Symphony* arrived as an epilogue to the whole series in 1915, the year of Griffith's *The Birth of a Nation*. It featured a sunrise, ascent, waterfall, view from the summit, thunderstorm, and descent (in retrograde motion). At one early performance, an assistant stood onstage and, as the *Musical Times* noted, "diligently exhibited numbers corresponding to the explanations in the programme, so that no one should mistake the glacier for the thermos flask." But by that time it was clear to everyone that the movies had usurped the aesthetic function of the tone poem. Strauss,

who had seen the handwriting on the concert-hall wall, wisely moved from there to the opera house and spent most of the next forty years of his career writing operas—among them *Salome* and *Der Rosenkavalier*. But in the last works that he wrote before his death at eighty-five, in 1949, he suddenly reverted to classical principles: his *Symphony for Winds* is dedicated to Mozart's "undying spirit, at the close of a life filled with gratitude."

Gustav Mahler was Strauss's only serious rival as a master of the post-Wagnerian orchestra. His scoring is as complex and expansive, but far more transparent in texture and less literal in its message. Mahler is a symbolist rather than a realist, and his music is fundamentally inner directed. He belongs, in fact, to the extraordinary epoch of Viennese cultural life that produced Hugo von Hofmannsthal, Karl Kraus, Egon Schiele, Oskar Kokoschka, and, above all, Gustav Klimt, whose glittering golden impastos and sinuous arabesques make the perfect visual counterpart to Mahler's symphonies.

Mahler was also a contemporary and compatriot of Sigmund Freud, and it is not too much to say that he wrote the first Freudian music—at least in the sense that he was the first to be consciously concerned with the workings of the subconscious in art. He did, in fact, have the benefit of a single psychoanalytic session with Freud during the summer of 1910, when the good doctor spent the whole of an afternoon analyzing what he diagnosed as Mahler's "mother fixation." It was a remarkably successful session. Mahler had been having trouble with his wife, Alma —had "withdrawn his libido from her," in Freud's phrase—but on the way home he already felt sufficiently recovered to write her a long love poem. Freud, for his part, was deeply impressed by Mahler's intuitive grasp of what was involved in psychoanalysis. "I had plenty of opportunity," he told Theodore Reik, "to admire the capability for psychological understanding of this man of genius."

Mahler had arrived at some Freudian insights long before he actually met the founder of psychoanalysis. Gifted with a neurotic's talent for self-analysis, he had already discovered the unconscious within himself and observed its effects on his music. "In the creative arts," he said, "virtually the only impressions that are fruitful and decisive in the long run are those that occur between the ages of four and eleven . . . anything later than that is rarely turned into art."

In his own symphonies and songs he always alluded to the tunes he had heard as a small boy. There was something fiercely compulsive about the way he kept reverting to his earliest memories as though, despite his technical perfection, he was trapped in the charmed circle of his childhood. What complicates Mahler's case is that his first impressions were of military marches and beerhall ditties, since he was brought up in a Czech garrison town where nothing else was available. As the story goes, "whenever little Gustav could not be found at home, it was certain he had gone marching off with some regiment, or else he might be standing on a coffee-house table, singing his songs for a throng of customers."

Growing up at the edge of a parade ground, he developed a lasting love-hate for the Austro-German marching band. Nearly all the Mahler

symphonies have at least one full-blown march movement—a funeral march, a mock-triumphal procession, or a march to the scaffold. At other times, often just at the most lyrical moments, he will suddenly launch into a savage parody of the old parade music, the drums lurching drunkenly, the brasses contorted into an agonized grimace. This penchant for barrack-room music was bound to annoy the critics of his day. As yet deaf to the possibilities of surrealism in music, they were almost unanimous in condemning his work as arid, banal, vulgar, derivative. "One wonders," wrote one critic, "whether indeed there has ever been a respectable composer who has utilized ideas as platitudinous [as these]. . . ."

But Mahler's platitudes belong to a special order of banality. He can take a vulgar scrap of melody, hold it up for inspection in the trumpets, deliver an ironic commentary in the horns, and fling it aside with a stifled curse from the kettledrums. (One of his most striking innovations was the use of brasses, rather than strings, as his principal melody instruments.) Working with two such tunes against the middle, he arrives at a new harmonic principle—dissonance by collision. More recent composers have written music that is much more densely dissonant than his. But perhaps no dissonances are quite as sharp and exciting as those that result when a seemingly predictable succession of consonances is suddenly derailed.

Mahler's youth was marked by a long series of tragic experiences, some of them afterward reflected in his *Kindertotenlieder* ("Songs on the Deaths of Children"). He came from a poor Jewish family in which only three of the twelve children lived to maturity. In later years, even after his rise to fame and his conversion to Catholicism, he referred to himself as a thrice homeless man: "as a Bohemian among Austrians, as an Austrian among Germans, and as a Jew among the peoples of the whole world." His "golden decade" as artistic director of the Vienna Opera, 1897–1907, established him as the foremost conductor of the day. His orchestras, by turns "alarmed and fascinated," always played better for him than they ever had before. "Mahler, in aspect and gesture, seemed at once genius and demon," wrote the conductor Bruno Walter, who became one of his assistants when he was only eighteen. "Never had I encountered so intense a human being. . . ." He went to New York to conduct at the Metropolitan Opera, and then took over the directorship of the New York Philharmonic. But he was already suffering from a severe cardiac ailment. After he collapsed during his forty-seventh concert of the 1911 season, he was rushed to Europe for medical attention, only to die in a Viennese sanatorium.

Mahler's conducting assignments never left him time enough to write his own music. Like Borodin, he called himself a *Sommerkomponist*, for nearly all his works were written during his summer holidays, when he could escape "this terrible treadmill of the theater" and spend his days in rural Austria, "roaming over mountains and through forests, and carrying off my day's bag of sketches. . . ." Once, when Bruno Walter went to visit him in Steinbach, on the Attersee, and stopped to admire the mountain scenery, Mahler told him: "Don't bother to look—I've composed all this already."

Conducting during the winter and composing only during summer vacations, Gustav Mahler (left) struggled to find time for his large-scale symphonies and his songs; below, the cover of his most tragic cycle of songs, the Kindertotenlieder. *The symbolic painting at right, by Klimt, matches the music of Mahler in giving a sense of the period's tension.*

He drew vast, cosmic conclusions from his annual encounters with the Alps, and the symphonic results are sometimes maddeningly metaphysical. In the Second Symphony, a huge fresco of death and immortality culminates in the great choral cry "Resurrection!" The Third Symphony is a hymn to nature nearly two hours long that includes "Summer Marching In" and reveals, among other things, "What the Flowers in the Meadow Tell Me." The Fourth Symphony presents a child's-eye view of paradise, based on an old peasant rhyme about the heavenly joys. The Eighth, the so-called Symphony of a Thousand, is nothing less than a gargantuan ceremonial for up to eleven hundred singers and instrumentalists (shades of Hector Berlioz!) that combines a medieval Latin hymn with Goethe's intimations of immortality from the final scene of *Faust*. "The symphony must be like the world," he once told Jean Sibelius. "It must embrace everything."

If Mahler had done no more than this—harangue the world on the beauties of faith and nature—he would probably be a forgotten composer. But Mahler's metaphysics have become secondary and expendable. His posthumous reputation, never higher than in the 1970's, rests on the fact that modern audiences have learned to value him for other things. His sarcasm is one of the saving graces—the curious way in which his music mocks and parodies in its own highest aspirations. His greatest discovery was the possibility of a new ambivalence in music. There had never been anything like it before, this polyphony of sonic ideas, this sense of music moving on several different levels of meaning at the same time. It was surrealism: not the small-scale surrealism of the fur-lined teacup, but oversize and magnificent in scale—the stream-of-consciousness in march time. Perhaps what he said about paradise is negligible, but he spoke all the more eloquently about the life of the unconscious self and the human condition. Never was a more brilliant technique placed at the service of a more fascinating neurosis. It was fortunate that Dr. Freud came too late to cure him of it.

9

Innovation and Revolution

ON MAY 29, 1913, AT THE NEWLY inaugurated Théâtre du Champs-Elysées, Sergei Diaghilev's Ballet Russe presented the première of Igor Stravinsky's *Le Sacre du Printemps* ("The Rite of Spring") before an audience composed of the most elegant women, the most fashionable young people, the most famous artists, the richest financiers, and the most arrant snobs in Paris. They had come to see the ballet, but what they got was a battle. No sooner had the performance begun than the first skirmishes erupted in the theater. "People laughed, scoffed, whistled, hissed and imitated animal noises," wrote the poet Jean Cocteau, who was in the thick of it. "They might eventually have tired themselves out had not the crowd of aesthetes and a few musicians, carried away by their excessive zeal, insulted and even roughly handled the public in the loges. The uproar degenerated into a fight."

Standing in her box, her tiara askew, the dowager Countess de Pourtalès flourished her fan and shouted, "It's the first time in sixty years that anyone has dared to make a fool of me!" Maurice Ravel, who had come to hear his colleague's work, politely requested a resplendently dressed neighbor to be quiet and was roundly abused for his pains. But the Beautiful People were divided in their sympathies. One society woman spat in the face of a demonstrator; another slapped the face of a man who was hissing in the next box. Her escort rose, and cards were exchanged; a duel was to be arranged. "It was all incredibly fierce," reported the American writer and doyen of expatriates Gertrude Stein. "We could hear nothing. As a matter of fact, I never did hear any of the music. . . ."

Beneath layers of civilization called technology, or nationalism, or Christianity, stands a human being with relatively standard desires and fears. He is the pagan within, studied by Sigmund Freud, placed in a new outer medium by Albert Einstein, and greeted by the artists of the twentieth century with the dance. Matched at left with fragments of Igor Stravinsky's score for Le Sacre du Printemps, *Valentino Hugo's drawings for the première show a young woman dancing herself toward death—for she is to be the pagan sacrifice in "the rite of spring."*

Indeed, for most of the audience the noise drowned out the startling new sounds coming from the pit. The young conductor on the podium, Pierre Monteux, threw desperate glances at the director's box, but he had orders not to interrupt the performance under any circumstances. The manager of the theater, Gabriel Astruc, who had put up half a million francs to guarantee *Sacre* and the season, stood in the box shouting, "First listen, then hiss!" Beside him—and beside himself—was Diaghilev, the veteran impresario of the Ballet Russe, vainly pleading, "Please let them get on with the show!" Finally they ordered the house lights turned on in order to quiet the audience and to let the police pick out and eject the worst troublemakers.

The thirty-year-old composer of the ballet had left the auditorium at the first sign of trouble and had gone backstage to watch the uproar from the wings. In later years, he recalled that evening:

> I have never again been that angry. The music was so familiar to me; I loved it, and I could not understand why people who had not yet heard it wanted to protest in advance. ... For the rest of the performance I stood in the wings behind Nijinsky [the choreographer] holding the tails of his *frac*, while he stood on a chair shouting numbers to the dancers, like a coxswain.

Onstage, the dancers were performing a stylized version of a primitive fertility rite based on Stravinsky's own startling vision of a pagan ceremony: "sage elders, seated in a circle, watched a young girl dance herself to death. They were sacrificing her to propitiate the god of spring."

It was a ballet without the conventional love interest, ostensibly close to the dawn of civilization. Musically, too, it reverted to those primitive sources from which the performing arts had originally sprung: nature worship, the choric dance, the rhythm of tribal drums. In many of its episodes, Stravinsky's complex and sumptuous score employed the kind of percussion that would have been more familiar to an African tribal chief than a Parisian balletomane. There were pages, like those of Moussorgsky (who was one of Stravinsky's decisive influences), consisting of constantly shifting accents—2/8, 3/16, 2/16, 3/16, 2/8, 2/16, 3/16, and so on—and these were hammered out by a pair of timpanists and an assortment of lesser percussion. Here, for the first time, was the full application of those neopagan principles that were to lead classical music out of the nineteenth-century doldrums. Like Picasso's African-inspired painting *Les Demoiselles d'Avignon*, it was one of the aesthetic milestones of the century, a work so important as to be considered the birth certificate of contemporary music. As one French critic wrote, "We were dumbfounded, overwhelmed by this hurricane that had come from the depths of the ages and which had taken life by the roots."

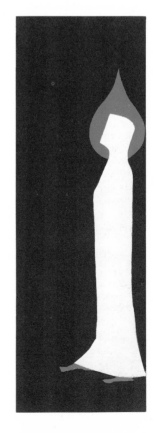

Both in its immediate impact and its long-range effect, *Sacre* proved to be one of the most influential works ever written. Somehow it crystallized the century's quest for a new sound, and soon there were dozens of composers who drew their own independent conclusions from Stravinsky's example. His Russian colleague Sergei Prokofiev, for example, composed a *Scythian Suite* that contains many of the same elements, including the sharp cutting edge of percussion and the pagan subject matter. "It is quite possible that I was now searching for the same images my own way," Prokofiev later admitted. Darius Milhaud, a leader of the Stravinskian French school known as *Les Six*, borrowed Brazilian jungle rhythms for his ballet *L'Homme et Son Désir* ("Man and His Desire"), for which he found the inspiration while serving in the French diplomatic service in Brazil during World War I. The chief of his mission, the poet-ambassador Paul Claudel, provided him with the ballet's scenario: "The principal character is Man, over whom the primitive forces have resumed their sway. ... And all the beasts, all the sounds of the everlasting forest come to gaze at him. ... And his dance

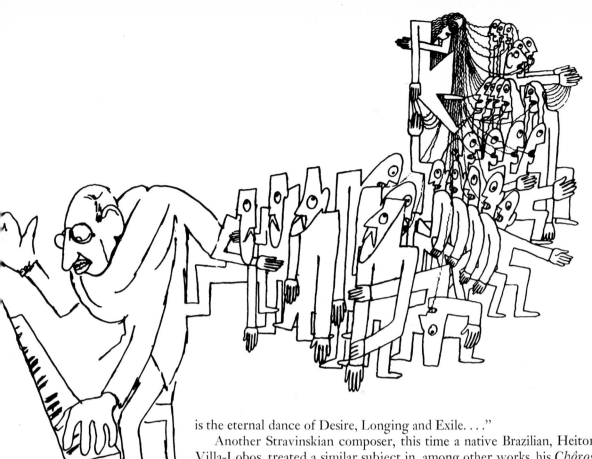

is the eternal dance of Desire, Longing and Exile. . . ."

Another Stravinskian composer, this time a native Brazilian, Heitor Villa-Lobos, treated a similar subject in, among other works, his *Chôros No. 10*, which depicts man's reaction to the valleys of the Amazon and the land of the Mato Grosso. The ballet *Appalachian Spring* by the American composer Aaron Copland is a more gentle, lyrical celebration of the same theme of the Eternal Return. Béla Bartók, who spent much of his youth hunting for primitive survivals in the peasant music of his native Hungary, perfected a "pagan" style of his own in works like *The Miraculous Mandarin* ballet or the Sonata for Two Pianos and Percussion. The piano itself turned into a sort of percussion instrument under the insistent "hammering" of his martellato style (beginning with the *Allegro Barbaro* of 1911)—an effect described by the English critic Percy Scholes as "A touch like a paving stone."

In one way or another these men all rediscovered something of the untapped energy that had previously been expressed only in works of primitive art. Yet now, in the midst of the twentieth century's aesthetic revolution, it was suddenly everywhere—in the violent colors of the Fauves, the "wild beasts" of French painting; in the jagged lines and fractured planes of the cubists; the pipeline-and-girder art of Fernand Léger; the number-and-alphabet poetry of Dada; the transposed images of the surrealists. There was a new poetry and a new prose—T. S. Eliot's *The Waste Land*, James Joyce's *Ulysses*, Guillaume Apollinaire's *Le Poète Assassiné*, Franz Kafka's *The Trial*. It was as though the release of energy in the arts was intended to keep pace with the new physics of Albert Einstein ($E=mc^2$) and the new psychiatry of Sigmund Freud.

Indeed, the throbbing rhythms of Stravinsky's work seemed just as appropriate for the machine age as for the primitive forces of pagan ritual. The Swiss composer Arthur Honegger, another prominent

133

member of *Les Six*, wrote a *Sacre*-inspired paean to "the visual impression and the physical sensation" of a 300-ton locomotive, *Pacific 231*, hurtling down the track at 120 miles an hour, "an intelligent monster, a joyous giant!" Still another "Son of *Sacre*" is Edgar Varése's *Ionisation* of 1931, which takes a molecular process as its point of departure and has thirteen orchestra players manipulating thirty-seven percussion instruments, including two sirens (one high, one low), two tam-tams, a gong, crash cymbals, three different sizes of bass drum, guiro (dessicated gourds with serrated surfaces designed to be rasped with a stick), slapsticks, Chinese blocks in three registers, claves, triangle, maracas, sleigh bells, castanets, tambourine, two anvils, chimes, celesta, and piano. The pianist, it should be added, plays with his forearms. And the result is as brilliant and exciting a piece of music as has ever been created by more conventional means.

Curiously enough, for all of *Sacre*'s far-reaching influence, Stravinsky himself never returned to the junglelike luxuriance of his early ballet style. He had already written two great "Russian" ballets, *The Firebird* and *Petrouchka*, in which the influence of his teacher, Rimsky-Korsakov, can still be detected. *Sacre* was the third and last. Thus, what was a beginning for so many others became, for Stravinsky, an ending. While waiting for *Sacre* to be produced he was already plot-

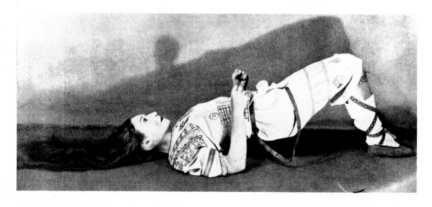

ting *Les Noces* ("The Wedding"), a work as cerebral and astringent as the other is full blooded and sensuous. From there his path led by quick steps to an almost monastic asceticism of sound—to "white" ballets like *Apollon Musagète*, and to the still more Apollonian *Agon*.

En route he made a series of fascinating experiments in neoclassicism, which involved composing like a twentieth-century Bach or a sort of modern Mozart. His Symphony in Three Movements, for example, is like a dissonant paraphrase of Beehoven; his Symphony in C was written under the sign of Haydn; an oratorio, *Oedipus Rex*, bears a family resemblance to Handel's oratorios, and an opera, *The Rake's Progress*, owes much of its form and inspiration to Mozart. The resulting style, of course, was always unmistakably Stravinskian in its astringent harmony, nervous rhythm, and tightly controlled form; he called it his "strong-bar-line music." He became a master of musical irony and often wrote pieces that were breezy and whimsical, such as his 1937 *Jeu*

Even bound, the tormented virgin of Le Sacre du Printemps *(left, below) continued to dance to Stravinsky's revolutionary score, subtitled* Scenes from Pagan Russia. *Considered by some as the Bach of our time in that he represents the last and the best of the "old" music, Stravinsky (left), turned in his later years at midcentury to the "new" twelve-tone serial music of Arnold Schoenberg (below).*

de Cartes, a ballet "in three deals" about a poker game. After he came to America in 1940 as an emigré from Hitler's Europe, he even composed a *Circus Polka* for the baby elephants of the Ringling Brothers and Barnum & Bailey Circus.

In his later years, however, Stravinsky came steadily closer to a taciturn, austere kind of music that sounds as though it were just a step away from silence. When he was already in his seventies, and living in Beverly Hills, California, he experimented for the first time with the complex twelve-tone technique that had been developed more than thirty years before by Arnold Schoenberg in Vienna.

Schoenberg himself was then a refugee, and living nearby in California, but there was no question of personal contact between the two composers. They met face to face only once during their years of exile, at the funeral of the refugee novelist Franz Werfel. "I have never found the music of this composer sympathetic, but it has interesting things," was Stravinsky's laconic way of summing up his attitude toward Schoenberg's work. What he disliked was its rhythmic shapelessness and the fact that it was "heavily founded in the most turgid and graceless Brahms." Still there was no escaping the influence of this extraordinary theorist whom many considered the greatest teacher of the century. Stravinsky ended up adapting Schoenberg's methods to many of his own late works—the *Canticum Sacrum* in honor of St. Mark the Apostle and the city of Venice (where, in 1971, Stravinsky was buried); the elegy *In Memoriam Dylan Thomas* ("Do Not Go Gentle Into That Good Night"); the ballet *Agon*, with its dance rhythms derived from French Renaissance music; and above all the *Threni* of 1957–58. This work, based on the Lamentations of Jeremiah, is a major score for orchestra, chorus, and soloists entirely constructed on a twelve-tone series.

These twelve-tone works (Stravinsky preferred to call them "a music of intervals") had the effect of healing the great ideological schism that had so long divided the world of modern music between the rival Schoenberg and Stravinsky factions. The whole controversy as to "schools" and "systems," which had seemed so important during the 1920's and 1930's and had caused so much bad feeling at the avantgarde music festivals, was now resolved at last. In retrospect, it seems as much a tempest in a teapot as the Brahms-Wagner feud. Schoenberg's ideals in music had always been very different from Stravinsky's, although he was no less of a revolutionary. He belonged to the German expressionist generation, which had put the scream onstage and turned *Angst* and anguish into art (as Schoenberg did in *Erwartung*, his monologue-opera about a woman waiting for a lover who turns up as a corpse). His essential rhythm was not that of the tribal drum but of the palpitating heart.

Intent on imposing a new order on the chaos of postromantic harmony, Schoenberg and his disciples arrived first at atonality, in which the chord relationships were deliberately so vague that no one could say what key a work was in, and then at the famous twelve-tone system, or as Schoenberg liked to call it, his "method of composition with twelve tones related only to one another." Briefly, this theory

rests on the fact that in traditional triadic harmony, the repetition of the predominant notes of a scale pulls the ear toward certain centers of tonal gravity. The gravitational attraction can be overcome only if no note in the scale is repeated until all others have been sounded, in some preordained series or "tone row" so that all have "equal rights." The result is the aural equivalent of weightlessness, and the harmony is divorced from its traditional associations.

Although the critics almost unanimously attacked the method as producing "ersatz" and "paper" music, Schoenberg always insisted that it was not nearly as forbidding as it looked. "It is primarily a method demanding logical order and organization." Besides, what really mattered to him was the fact that he had created a new sound, *ein neuer Klang*. "A new sound is an unintentionally discovered symbol which proclaims the new man who utters it," he wrote in his great textbook on *Harmonielehre*, the theory of harmony.

Like Stravinsky, Schoenberg had enjoyed considerably more success with his early, more conventional works than with his later "cerebral" music. His youthful tone poem *Verklärte Nacht* ("Transfigured Night") had established his reputation in Vienna as a master in the Wagner-Mahler tradition, and his *Gurre-Lieder* song cycle was hailed as "the finest musical love poem since Tristan." After he had begun dispensing with tonality and tonal centers, however, there were protests and disturbances at virtually all the Schoenberg premières. At the 1907 debut of his First String Quartet, for example, the audience made a rush for the doors in the middle of the piece; one especially waggish listener led the way out through the emergency exit. Gustav Mahler was in the audience that night, doing his best to restore order, and history records a memorable exchange between Mahler and a demonstrator: Mahler, in a high dudgeon, exclaimed, "You have not to hiss!" The demonstrator shouted back defiantly, "I also hiss at your symphonies!"

Throughout his subsequent career, Schoenberg was exposed to an incredible amount of vituperation from critics and detractors. He was attacked as a fake, an anarchist, a madman; Richard Strauss suggested that "only a psychiatrist can help poor Schoenberg now." The composer wrote that he could not understand what he had done to make them so violent and aggressive—"I am still certain that I never took anything from them which was theirs." But in any case, none of the adverse criticism was ever able to shake his impenetrable sangfroid: "I write the kind of music which does not appeal to those who understand nothing about it. But one must admit that it appeals to those who understand it."

Schoenberg's work on his vast twelve-tone opera *Moses und Aron* was interrupted in 1933, when the Nazis came to power in Germany. Although an Austrian, he had been made a professor and member of the Prussian Academy of the Arts in Berlin. But when the president of the academy told a meeting of the membership that he had been ordered to destroy the "Jewish influence" there, Schoenberg rose to say that he never stayed where he was not wanted, and walked out. He and his family went to America, where he accepted another teaching post at the University of California at Los Angeles. Whatever it was in the

Arnold Schoenberg died in 1951 before completing his opera Moses und Aron, *but it has, nevertheless, been performed; the poster at right announces a 1960 Berlin production. Schoenberg left two life-long disciples: Anton von Webern (below, right), who developed a musical language from the syntactic rules left by Schoenberg, and Alban Berg, whose masterful opera* Wozzeck, *advertised below, relates the story of a victimized Austrian soldier.*

California air that turned Stravinsky into a Schoenbergian of sorts also turned Schoenberg into a Stravinskian in some of his later works, which revert to the old tonal harmony of his youth. "In me, too, the fervid wish for tonal harmonies frequently arises," he explained, "and then I must surrender to this urge. After all, composing means obeying an inner compulsion."

Even so, Schoenberg went on refining and expanding the twelve-tone method. One of his better-known American scores is the Piano Concerto, Opus 42, whose significance he once tried to explain to Oscar Levant with the program note: "Life was so easy; suddenly hatred broke out (Presto), a grave situation was created (Adagio). But life goes on (Rondo)." His last piece of dramatic music was composed in 1947. Scored for narrator, men's chorus, and orchestra, *A Survivor from Warsaw* presents a single incident from the massacre of the Polish Jews under the Nazi occupation—a brief, flickering vision of terror like the sudden opening of the doors to an inferno. "This text is based partly upon reports which I have received directly or indirectly," he noted grimly on the manuscript. It forms the tragic fulfillment of the premonitions contained in the *Angsttraum* ("fear dream") compositions of his early expressionism. And only then, with this final work, did it become apparent to most of the critics that no other style could have done justice to such a subject and that the twelve-tone method was the ideal way of dealing musically with the psychopathology of the twentieth century.

When Schoenberg died in 1951, at the age of seventy-eight, he had outlived both of his most famous disciples, Alban Berg and Anton Webern, who had applied his methods to other kinds of musical problems. Berg was a lyrical twelve-tone composer with a special interest in the expressionist theater. His opera *Wozzeck*, based on George Büchner's play about a half-demented soldier, achieved the stature of a classic soon after its 1928 première. And it is now one of the most frequently performed of all modern operas—proving that, under some circumstances, the Schoenberg technique could appeal to mass audiences as well as intellectuals.

Webern, on the other hand, was a sort of physicist or a mathematician-composer. He devoted a lifetime to writing epigrammatic songs and pieces, some less than a minute long. Taken all together, they total less than three hours, or barely enough to fill four LP records. He was the supreme master of musical compression, as Schoenberg was well aware when he wrote the foreword to Webern's Six Bagatelles for String Quartet: "Any glance can be stretched into a poem, any sight into a novel. But to express a novel in a single gesture, a destiny in a single breath—such concentration can only be found where there is a corresponding lack of sentimentality."

Webern's slender pieces were banned by the Nazis as "degenerate art," although he himself was allowed to go on living inconspicuously in Vienna during the war. Then, in 1945, he was accidentally shot and killed by an American soldier during the arrest of a blackmarketeer, and it seemed for a time as though his very unobtrusive music would die with him. Yet within a decade his works had emerged from obscurity, and he was suddenly regarded as one of the two or three most vital influences on the next generation of contemporary composers— notably Pierre Boulez in France, Karlheinz Stockhausen in Germany, and Luigi Nono in Italy.

This same generation of postwar modernists also discovered another major figure whose works had been habitually neglected, Edgar Varèse. Born and educated in France, Varèse had come to America after World War I and had attracted considerable attention with his experimental scores of the 1920's and 1930's, especially *Ionisation*, *Intégrales*, and *Amériques*. Yet for the most part he was jealously excluded from the "official" musical life of New York until it became apparent, in the 1950's, that he had anticipated the whole development of *musique concrète* by writing what was, in effect, "electronic" music before the electronic means for it had even been invented.

As a young man, Varèse had been a protégé of Debussy and Richard Strauss, but he soon became famous—or better said, notorious —as the most scientifically minded of avant-garde composers. When he was in his sixties and seventies, and tape recorders had become available at last, his studio in New York City's Greenwich Village resembled a sonic laboratory rather than the conventional music room. In it he recorded, edited, filtered, and re-composed the whole *cante jondo* of modern civilization, from drill presses to carborundum wheels. "Webern liberated silence, but Varèse emancipated noise," observed a German critic. In *Deserts*, of 1954, he combined a group of live musi-

Edgar Varèse (above) was seventy-five years old in 1958 when his tape Poème Electronique *was played to audiences in Le Corbusier's Phillips Pavilion (right) at that year's Brussels Exposition. As images were projected on a screen (far right) audiences listened—although the naturalized American composer generally preferred to isolate sound from other experiences. His flute solo* Density 21.5, *for instance, explores the sounds possible to produce upon the new platinum (a metal with a specific density of 21.45) flute.*

cians with a set of taped sound-tracks so as to evoke "all physical deserts (of sand, sea, snow, of outer space, of empty city streets), but also the deserts in the mind of man; not only those stripped aspects of nature that suggest bareness, aloofness, timelessness, but also that remote inner space no telescope can reach, where man is alone, a world of mystery and essential loneliness."

Later, for the Brussels World's Fair of 1958, he did away with human musician-intermediaries altogether and composed a *Poème Électronique* entirely on tape. Composed for Le Corbusier's parabolic Phillips Pavilion, it was designed to sweep in continuous arcs of sound through something like four hundred loudspeakers. Before his death in 1965, at the age of eighty, Varèse was at least able to enjoy some of the pleasures of belated recognition—the satisfaction of seeing the light of comprehension going on here and there, at the modern music festivals and in the universities.

Varèse's remarkable career had encompassed the whole of the modernist revolution, from *Pelléas et Mélisande* to electronic computer music. Somehow his work best sums up the tremendous changes that had taken place in "art music" within little more than half a century—changes hardly less momentous in the arts than those that had meanwhile taken place in the sciences, or indeed in the quality of life itself. Perhaps more keenly than any other composer of his day, Varèse understood how important it was for the arts to keep up with the times. He used to carry in his pocket a slip of paper with an admonitory quotation from Albert Einstein that he would declaim at appropriate moments. "Our actual situation cannot be compared with anything in the past," it said. "We must radically change our way of thinking, our method of action."

10

The Once and Future Music

DUKE ELLINGTON, BURT BACHARACH, Loretta Lynn, Lightning Hopkins, Elvis Presley, Leonard Bernstein, Ray Charles, The Rolling Stones, Luciano Berio, Bob Dylan, B. B. King, Frank Zappa, Cat Stevens, Aretha Franklin—these are a few of the prominent musicians of the latter third of the twentieth century, and their names are symbolic of the "many mansions" that comprise the house of music in the age of electronic communication. Never before has there been so much music available to so vast an audience, or such a multiplicity of ways for human beings to express their musical impulses—jazz, folk, soul, rock, pop, country and western, symphonic and "light classical," Broadway and Hollywood, serious and trivial. This bewildering profusion of styles is evidence of a great revolution in the art of organizing sounds. The old conventions are suddenly no more. The forms and purposes of music are in a state of flux; no one seems at all certain where music might be heading next.

A generation after the introduction of the tape recorder and the LP record, the full impact of electronic technology begins to be felt both in the production and consumption of music. Now that it is no longer necessary to have a hundred-man symphony orchestra in order to produce a sound loud enough to fill an auditorium, the emphasis has shifted to individual expression by soloists and "chamber" groups, such as the pop combination of singer, guitars, organ, bass, and percussion.

No less important is the fact that music of all epochs, countries, and styles is now available on tapes or discs, so that every music lover is free to exercise his options continually, and with a far wider choice of material than even the greatest of the old music patrons of Versailles or Esterháza would ever have dreamed of. A not untypical record collection might range from Monteverdi madrigals and Corelli concertos to Bach, Berlioz, and Bartók, Tibetan monks chanting mantras, Carlos Montoya playing flamenco guitar, Erroll Garner on the piano, Muddy Waters singing the blues, Ravi Shankar playing the sitar. In short, the age of total eclecticism is upon us. By the same token there is no longer a single prevailing taste in contemporary art music, which ranges all the way from relatively traditionalist works by composers like Benjamin Britten, to the fragmentations of Karlheinz Stockhausen, the tape-loop constructions of Terry Riley, and the "indeterminacy" experiments of John Cage. The picture may appear hopelessly unfocused, yet there are

If music had gone as far as it could go with Stravinsky's conversion to serialism, rock fans of the second half of the century neglected to mourn and turned to their own form of rejoicing: at left a rock organist stays in electronic touch with his Mannheim, Germany, audience.

forces at work to bring about an eventual reconciliation between the competing worlds of pop and avant-garde—a synthesis foreshadowed in the later Beatle records and in some of the more adventurous film scores.

Despite the fragmentation and the contradictions, there is one thing that all modern music has in common: every style, without exception, has been profoundly influenced by the convergence of the two great mainstreams, African rhythm and European harmony, which first occurred in America and has since spread to the rest of the world. This fusion of elements is probably the most significant musical development of the last hundred years, comparable in importance to the birth of counterpoint or the romantic revolution.

Yet it was a slow process that occurred spontaneously and often against determined opposition from the guardians of musical taste. Then, before anyone quite realized what was happening, a new sound welled up out of the former colonial countries where black and white had long been, if not on equal terms, at least within earshot of each other. And an astonished world suddenly found itself listening and moving to Dixieland, the blues, the foxtrot, the conga, the mambo, the Lindy Hop, be bop, bossa nova, soul, rock. "The plaintive and derisive songs of an oppressed people," noted the British anthropologist Geoffrey Gorer, "have become the background for a whole society's pleasures and distractions." But the influence went deeper than that. Within the last fifty years, Afro-American rhythms have altered the world's conception of how music ought to sound. As one European concert pianist expressed it, "Once you hear how the blacks move in music, you never want to go back to the old way."

In the United States, musical integration has been a continuous process going back to Colonial days. Although the African slaves were often denied the right to use their drums—their masters feared, perhaps rightly, that the drums would spark insurrections—they were allowed to go on singing and playing stringed instruments. Often they displayed such a genius for music that anyone with a trained ear was

Diaghilev sensed that the approach to the twentieth-century pagan was through dance, and jazz with its sophisticated African rhythms always spoke to the body and made it move. Below is Joe "King" Oliver's dance band with its witty virtuoso trumpeter, Louis Armstrong, standing at left; at right, above, gospel singers clap in a production of The Trumpets of the Lord.

bound to take notice, and many white men were deeply impressed. It was on account of the blacks' singing that the white planters were first obliged to recognize the humanity of their "savage" slaves. The slave-owning, violin-playing Thomas Jefferson even had the temerity to suggest, in his *Notes on Virginia*, that black men were superior to white men in this respect: "In music they are generally more gifted than the whites," he wrote, "with accurate ears for tune and time."

European musicians who came into contact with the slaves often reached the same conclusion. The famous English actress and singer Fanny Kemble, in her *Journal of a Residence on a Georgia Plantation*, confesses herself profoundly moved by the singing she heard among the slaves in the 1830's: "The high voices all in unison, and the admirable time and true accent with which their responses are made, make me wish that some great musical composer would hear these ... performances. With a very little skillful adaptation and instrumentation [they] would make the fortune of an opera." The great Viennese pianist Henri Herz came to America from Paris in the 1840's and fell in love with the "solemn, resonant and harmonious" notes of the black banjo players he heard during his tour of the South. Herz wrote of the music he heard:

> Negroes are very appreciative of music, and their souls are far from being closed to the beauties of poetry. A collection of their songs has been made, and a study of it reveals an uncommon tenderness and rigorous observance of the laws of rhythm, that elemental core of all music, so well known to everyone, and yet so difficult to explain. From time to time, while listening to Negro banjo players, I have pondered the mysterious law of rhythm which seems to be a universal law, since rhythm is coordinated movement, and movement is life, and life fills the universe.

Louis Moreau Gottschalk, the first American-born composer of international importance, made his reputation in the mid-nineteenth century with a series of piano pieces based on black music from Louisiana and the Caribbean, with its mixture of French, Spanish, and African

145

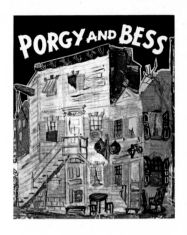

elements. During the 1890's, when the Bohemian composer Antonin Dvořák came to teach at the American Conservatory in New York, it was again the Negro spirituals that made the most lasting impression on him: indeed, a paraphrase of "Swing Low, Sweet Chariot" found its way into the *New World Symphony* (it had been among the plantation songs sung for him by his black pupil, Henry Burleigh).

Dvořák told his students that "the future music of this country must be founded upon what are called the Negro melodies." And in a long article published in *Harper's* magazine, he wrote that black music was already "unconsciously recognized as their own" by most Americans: "What songs, then, belong to the American and appeal more strongly to him than any others? What melody could stop him on the street if he were in a strange land and make the home feeling well up within him, no matter how hardened he might be or how wretchedly the tune were played?" This reads like a scenario for George Gershwin's *An American in Paris*, where a blues melody is introduced to underscore the hero's homesickness. It was as though Dvořák had foreseen that thirty or forty years hence, the jazz descendants of his "plantation melodies" would in fact sound the keynote for American culture.

Gershwin, as it happens, was one of the first composers to try his hand at symphonic jazz. His best-known effort in this direction, the *Rhapsody in Blue*, was perhaps less successful in "making a lady out of jazz" (as the saying went) than in creating a concert framework for the Broadway pseudo-jazz of which he was then the world's leading exponent, and which was in itself a melange of black and white elements. Gershwin was a brilliantly gifted master of the idiom: "I Got Rhythm," "The Man I Love," "That Certain Feeling," "Someone to Watch over Me," and the rest are to the American repertoire what Franz Schubert's songs were to the German Lied. But his most successful use of black folklore was in *Porgy and Bess*, an all-black opera about the inhabitants of Catfish Row in Charleston, South Carolina.

In 1934, while Gershwin was at work on the score, he and his librettist, Dubose Heyward, spent a summer doing background research among the black farmers of the Carolina sea islands. At that time there were still some African musical survivals in these isolated communities, including the singing technique called "shouting," which Heyward described as "a complicated rhythmic pattern beaten out by feet and hands as an accompaniment to the spirituals." Gershwin, who soon learned how to take part in the "shouting," steeped himself in the local music just as Moussorgsky had when he went to live among the Russian peasants in preparation for *Boris Godunov*. Heyward recalled an experience he and Gershwin had one evening:

> ... as we were about to enter a dilapidated cabin that had been taken as a meeting house by a group of Negro Holy Rollers, George caught my arm and held me. The sound that had arrested him ... consisted of perhaps a dozen voices raised in loud rhythmic prayer. The odd thing about it was that while each had started at a different time, upon a different theme, they formed a clearly defined rhythmic pattern, and that this, with the actual words lost, and the inevitable pounding of the rhythm, produced an effect almost terrifying in its primitive intensity.

Ella, Louis—both the blues and jazz were personal, rising like easy, sometimes secret, conversations from the lives of America's blacks. Above: the cover of a Porgy and Bess *program from the works of the jazz student George Gershwin; at right, a lithograph entitled* Jazz Birth *depicts a scene from the rural South; below left, Ella Fitzgerald singing the blues, and right, Armstrong takes off on a trumpet improvisation while holding his familiar white handkerchief.*

For Gershwin this experience led directly to the storm scene of *Porgy and Bess* in which six simultaneous prayers rise above the fury of an orchestral hurricane. But the whole episode serves as a perfect illustration of the rhythmic (and melodic) inspiration that black musicians invariably brought to white music—not only at the operatic level but at every point of cultural contact.

Although Heyward, like many other writers, uses the word "primitive" to describe this music, technically speaking African rhythm is anything but that—as anyone who has ever tried to write it down will testify. It involves several highly sophisticated techniques that are evidently the product of an ancient tradition of rhythmic interplay, such as can take place only in close-knit tribal communities. The results are far more flexible and exciting than anything to be found in European rhythm. Inevitably, some of this elasticity was lost in the process of adjusting the African beat to the needs of a four-square harmonic pattern, yet enough freedom remained to lend rhythmic excitement to the early jazz styles. In most 1920's jazz, for example, a steady 1-2-3-4 beat in quick tempo supports one or two interlocking rhythms that break down the beat into smaller components and stress the offbeats; sometimes it is also instinctively "polyrhythmic," in that two or more entirely different rhythms may be moving along at the same time.

The question-and-answer character of so much Afro-American music has its origin in the antiphonal structure of African work songs and tribal chants, where the lead singer is answered by the massed voices of the other participants:

> It is crying, it is crying,
>   Sihamba Ngenyanga.
> The child of the walker by moonlight,
>   Sihamba Ngenyanga.
> It was done intentionally by people whose
>   names cannot be mentioned
>   Sihamba Ngenyanga.
> They sent her for water during the day,
>   Sihamba Ngenyanga.

When the African slaves were converted to Christianity in the new world, they went on singing in the same patterns. The typical spiritual is just as antiphonal as the African work song:

> Oh, the River of Jordan is deep and wide,
>   One more river to cross.
> I don't know how to get on the other side,
>   One more river to cross.
> Oh, you got Jesus, hold him fast,
>   One more river to cross.
> Oh, better love was never told,
>   One more river to cross.

The American blues, too, have their antecedents in African chants with a similar sort of construction: a steep rise in the melody, followed by a gentle "sloping down," followed by another steep rise and gentle, step-wise descent. Blues singers follow the African tradition of "vocalizing" the sound of their accompanying instruments by "teasing" the strings of a guitar with a knife or a bottle neck, for example, so that the tone becomes very elastic and responsive. And ethnomusicologists have noted the same penchant for "gapped pentatonic" scales among Mississippi bluesmen as among the tribal singers of West Africa.

A long and complex development led from the "hollers" and blues of the southern field hands to the full-blown Dixieland jazz bands that first rose to prominence at "$1.50 a couple" picnics outside of New Orleans. Later, the sound moved north with the riverboats. The first mention of jazz in the press is in a *Variety* story dated October 27, 1916:

> Chicago has added another innovation to its list of discoveries in the so-called 'Jazz Bands.' The Jazz Band is composed of three or more instruments and seldom plays regulated music. The College Inn and practically all the other high-class places of entertainment have a Jazz Band featured, while the low cost makes it possible for all the smaller places to carry their Jazz orchestra.

It was this strong, exuberant music, played by ear and bursting with vitality, that gave its name to the Jazz Age. Pure jazz, played largely by black musicians, gradually evolved into several distinct varieties, giving birth to be bop (which abandoned the old rhythmic framework) and modern jazz. Although it began as a folk idiom designed for dancing, it has developed into a complex form of instrumental "chamber music" intended simply to be listened to by audiences of connoisseurs comparable to those for classical music. In much diluted form, the jazz impulse inspired the swing bands of white musicians like Benny Goodman, as well as the swinging style of pop singers (also known as crooners) of the Bing Crosby-Frank Sinatra school. Meanwhile, jazz played an increasingly important role in serious music. Charles Ives, the Connecticut Yankee whose polytonal experiments had anticipated Stravinsky's, led the way by using ragtime rhythms at the turn of the century. Gershwin, Copland, and Bernstein were among the Americans who followed suit, while Ravel, Stravinsky, Hindemith, and Milhaud headed

From shouts in the work fields and from the tender gospel heritage of The Trumpets of the Lord *(right), black music moved through the New Orleans ensemble and the Chicago soloist style to the big band of Edward Kennedy "Duke" Ellington (below, left). The Duke's arrangements seemed more like improvisations than they actually were.*

the list of Europeans who set down their symphonic (and in some cases rather hilarious) impressions of what jazz sounded like to their ears.

The full impact of soul rhythm could be felt only after white popular music began to respond to the stimulus of "race records," alias rhythm and blues, and singers like Leadbelly (Huddie Ledbetter), Bessie Smith, and Billie Holiday. Elvis Presley and the rock 'n roll of the 1950's were part of the answer to this challenge. Then, in the 1960's, it was the Beatles' turn to launch a revolution in popular music. When they first appeared on the scene they sang like very young and energetic angels flapping wing-shaped guitars, with a hard-driving sound based on Memphis rock, British "skiffle" groups, and the Harlem blues. Only the texts of their songs belonged to the English music-hall tradition, and were thus closer to Bea Lillie than Leadbelly.

The words the Beatles sang were surprisingly bland, coming from an unruly generation whose taste for unabated high volume was blowing the roofs off the discothèques. Evidently the Beatles had got hold of some secret sorrow and made it articulate—"Don't be bad to me; hold me, love me; I call your name but you're not there; I'm a loser; did you have to treat me, oh, so bad?" (Perhaps it was the Oedipal drama of a generation that had undergone the trauma of permissive parenthood and demand feeding. When Lennon and McCartney pleaded, "don't go 'way; I'm afraid that I might miss you," they touched on the same emotional anguish that another British poet, A. A. Milne, had summed up so poignantly in the lines, "You must never go down/ to the end of the town/ without consulting me.")

In later Beatle records the focus shifted from second person accusative to third person feminine ("She's a Woman"), the accent stopped

The Beatles—John Lennon, Paul McCartney, Ringo Starr, and George Harrison—struck reverberating notes in their listeners; but there is no planned sound in 4'33" the famous silent work of John Cage (above). As the serialist composers abandon much of their control to a predetermined sequence of notes, Cage abandoned his in 4'33" to chance and to the audience, giving them only a time limit and an opened but silent piano.

coming down on the hard beats, and the twang of guitars was augmented by the palsied tones of the electronic organ. In "We Can Work It Out," echoes of a French music-hall musette broke like a thunderclap across a pop scene that had heard nothing but four-four time for a generation. It was as if the Beatles had independently invented waltz time (here disguised as triplets).

At about the same time, serious musicians made the discovery—discussed on television by Leonard Bernstein—that some of these tunes were nearly as modal as Gregorian chant. Yet it was hardly surprising that the Beatles should show the same preference for the Dorian mode and the pentatonic scale as the English folksongs and American blues from which their melodies derive. George Harrison learned to play an uncertain sitar in India and brought an Asian element into the arsenal of pop sounds. Soon they were borrowing sounds from everywhere: a horn obbligato from Schubert, a clarin trumpet from Bach (blowing fanfares for the fireman who likes to keep a clean machine), and for "Eleanor Rigby," a string accompaniment that bore a striking resemblance to the *Bachianas Brasileiras* of Villa Lobos.

"I don't like that kind of classical music. I can't stand it," McCartney explained to the underground *International Times.* "But it fitted, it was just lucky it fitted." Yet whether they wanted to or not, the Beatles had already breached the great wall between classical music and the pop world. Later, in "Sergeant Pepper," they unleashed a great orgy of free association that was related to the experiments of John Cage, the father of "random" musicmaking. Here the sound was composed of jangling harps, wheezing calliopes, Detroit soul rhythms, a choral fugato on "We shall scrimp and save," electric guitars going off like wobbly firecrackers, dogs barking, memories of Fred and Adele Astaire, and a Hindu-inspired chant about saving the world through love. There was even a forty-one-man symphony orchestra, raising a vast banshee wail and making a sound only slightly smaller than the one Mahler used in the *Symphony of a Thousand.*

Their talents were such that every record they touched turned to gold. They possessed an extraordinary power to sway the multitudes, and indeed, although the group itself has split up, their songs seem destined to go on forever. It was as if a whole society—not otherwise noted for its generosity to poets—had decided to subsidize its creative subconscious to the tune of twenty million dollars a year. And, whatever their fate as a group, the line of musical development the Beatles chose to follow is of vital importance to the further development of music. They were the first to demonstrate that pop and classical can be brought together in some musically meaningful way. If their eclecticism is pursued to its logical conclusion, it may be that the art of music will become a continuum once more instead of a series of independent and soundproof compartments. Perhaps, in the day of the "global village," that may not be too distant a prospect.

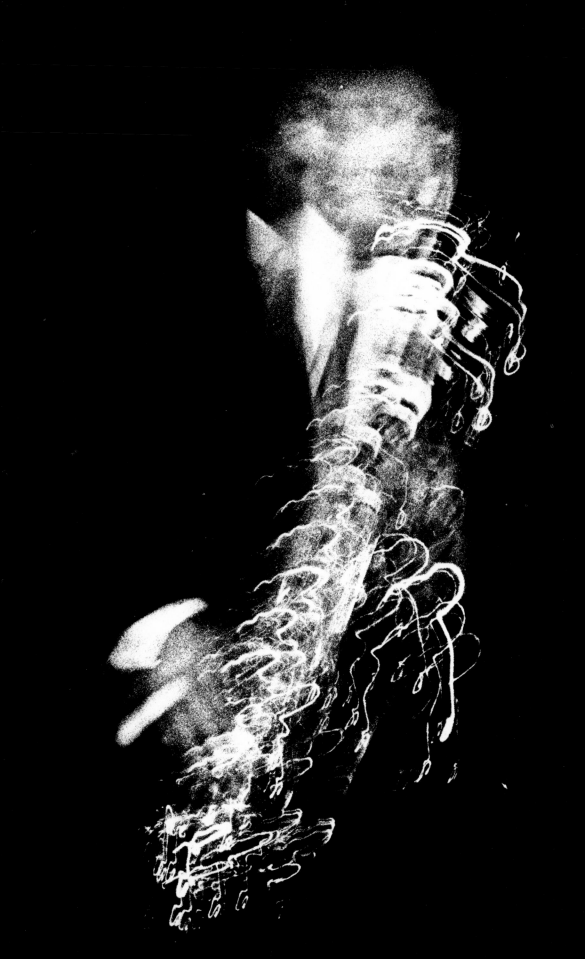

MEMOIRS OF
MUSICAL LIVES

Arturo Toscanini's concentration on the symphony orchestra began late in his career. But such was the brilliance of his technique that our perception of the conductor's role has been permanently altered as a result of his work. A profile of the maestro, written by Winthrop Sargeant while Toscanini was conductor of the NBC Symphony from 1937 to 1954, gives us an insight into his genius.

Thirty years ago, the name Arturo Toscanini referred to an able but relatively obscure and already middle-aged Italian opera conductor whose principal triumphs had been achieved in the orchestra pits at La Scala and the Metropolitan Opera House. Today, Arturo Toscanini is, without question, the most celebrated musician in the world. He is, with the possible exception of the Pope, the most famous living Italian. His reputation outshines those of nearly all the contemporary composers whose works he occasionally conducts. He is probably the highest-paid symphony conductor in the history of music. Musicians have reverently collected the splintered batons that he breaks and throws away when he is angry. One sentimental New York woman treasures a piece of ruptured paneling that he once broke when, in a temper, he thrust his fist through a door in his Carnegie Hall dressing room. Legends about his amazingly accurate ear and his phenomenal memory have approached the incredible. Not since Nicolò Paganini reputedly sold his soul to the devil for an E string has a prominent musician enjoyed such a reputation for uncanny, occult and mysterious power. In an age of virtuosos, when the symphonic conductor has become the king of virtuosos, Toscanini is the greatest virtuoso of them all.

The man thus prematurely immortalized is a sharp-eyed, white-haired, extremely wiry Italian whose bare five feet of height usually come as a surprise to those who meet him off the stage. He dresses with prim severity—nearly always in black. Socially he is surprisingly shy. He loves the company of pretty women and hugely enjoys an occasional evening at a Manhattan night club. But he always looks vaguely out of place in any gathering he cannot lead with a baton. He has a reputation for childish helplessness in practical affairs and is said to be incapable of finding his own collar buttons or getting his hair cut without the help of his sedate, capable-looking wife. But he is shrewd enough to bargain closely over his concert and broadcast fees. In private life he is alternately fussy and playful, headstrong in both his enthusiasms and hatreds, intolerant of anything in the way of opposition. To many, his celebrated encounters with Europe's Nazi and Fascist authorities have made him a symbol of democratic idealism. A fervent nationalist like most of his countrymen, he is politically an avowed and tested liberal. But Toscanini is, both professionally and by temperament, an absolute dictator. He is also deeply and matter-of-factly convinced that he is the greatest conductor in the world.

His arrival at Rockefeller Center in New York City for his weekly broadcasts is as carefully prepared as the official reception of a monarch. In his dressing room several dress suits, complete from tie to socks, are carefully laid out, awaiting his intermission rubdown and change of clothing. A bowl of watermelon balls, which he likes to eat following a concert, lies cooling for him in a refrigerator. Pictures of his wife and family and favorite composers, without which he will refuse to conduct, are tastefully arranged on his dressing table. A punctual half hour before broadcast time, Toscanini's chauffeur-driven Chevrolet arrives at the 49th Street entrance of the RCA Building from his rented home in Riverdale. Toscanini steps into an elevator and is carefully whisked to the eighth floor. The hundred men of the NBC Symphony, already seated and tuned up, are waiting in nervous silence. So is a hushed audience that has begged and bought, at fantastic black-market prices, the tickets that the National Broadcasting Company allots to a chosen few of the musical world. This audience, composed largely of connoisseurs, listens to the ensuing program with the most reverent attention, for it is, like all Toscanini programs, a unique experience. . . .

Toscanini's uncanny control of the orchestral machine rests largely on the fact that he is acutely aware of the work of each individual instrumentalist. Musicians know that the average conductor is easily satisfied with a general impression of puffed cheeks and active bow strokes. With Toscanini it is different. When a musician makes an effort he can see it register immediately on his imperious face. When the effort is not made, that fact registers also. And such is the maestro's keenness of ear that even the third double-bass player from the end feels like a goldfish in a bowl, his every groaning sixteenth-note under microscopic observation.

There are, however, compensations for the player who sweats under this omniscience. Toscanini has a way of intuitively sensing the potentialities, failings and even the momentary emotional status of the men who are playing under him. He seldom tyrannizes over a nervous man, and he never picks a flaw or throws a tantrum arbitrarily. Nor does he seek, as lesser conductors sometimes do, to bamboozle experienced orchestra players with meaningless and transparent sleight of hand in order to impress them with his knowledge. The knowledge, fortified by the famous Toscanini memory, is there. It needs no herald trumpeting to get itself noticed. Any mistake, except one due to carelessness or downright stupidity, generally meets with encouragement and patient drilling. Though he is relentless in exposing any laxity, the maestro's attitude toward the music and toward his men is one of open, almost childlike, sincerity. Moreover, orchestra players will tell you that it is actually more difficult to make a mistake under Toscanini than under any other conductor. His erratic, paddling beat is so enormously expressive that even an unimportant player who is temporarily at sea can tell, just by watching it, exactly where and how to make his entrances. . . .

Every rehearsal sees a thousand moods rise and subside in the "old man," a thousand ways of getting what he wants out of the hundred-odd men under him. Completely absorbed in his complicated task, he seems as transparent and unself-conscious as a four-year-old child gravely making mud pies. While he is conducting, he sings continuously—or rather, wails like a disembodied banshee—apparently quite oblivious to the fact that his piping, cracked-sounding voice can often be heard above the music. For a while he will play elegantly and delightedly with the delicate lacework of some Mozart or Haydn symphony. An exquisite sensual happiness will seem to permeate his whole being. Intolerant of the slightest imperfection in his toy, he will smooth out the air before him, stroking and shaping it into a symbol of elegant and polished sound. A sour note or a scratchy fiddle passage will overwhelm him with a desperate sense of disappointment which would move even a bass-drum player to remorse. For a moment anger will threaten. Unable to get what he wants by imperious methods, he will try wheedling it out of the players like a clever woman, or he will threaten to tear himself apart with hysterics if he is not appeased. Sometimes, like a possessed dervish he will take to praying and swearing, trying to bring forth a performance by a species of incantation. An obstinately repeated error will suddenly rouse him to furious sarcasm: "*Io credo* . . ." he will begin with fiery deliberation, "I think, that there is an accent over that F sharp. But," he will continue, biting off each word and glaring at the culprit, "I am only Toscanini, and I am probably wrong. *Vediamo!*" Calling for a copy of the score, he will rustle impatiently through the pages holding them within three or four inches of his nearsighted eyes. Then, finding the passage in question, he will elaborately pretend to be thunderstruck. "Ah, no *Signori*. Imagine. I am right! Mozart has written an accent there." With an impatient whip stroke and a murderous-sounding grunt, the scene will be finished and the culprit, who has been staring guiltily at the accent all the time, will thank his stars that his temporary moment in the spotlight is over. . . .

As geniuses go, Toscanini is not an enormously conceited man, and aside from moments of Napoleonic Latin imperiousness, he is certainly not a pompous one. Yet the maestro, like all authentic geniuses, has a deep sense of the importance of his extraordinary abilities. Perhaps this sense is better illustrated by another anecdote, which I can vouch for, as I was there when the event happened: Several years ago (in 1930, to be exact) on a train approaching Budapest, a cosmopolitan group of Philharmonic musicians sat in a compartment talking and drinking champagne. Their spirits were high. But their manners were respectfully restrained, and their conversation was relatively lofty. Their host was Toscanini. Usually affable and friendly in his off-duty moments, Toscanini had been smiling in his detached way, quietly discussing details of scoring and instrumental technique, gesticulating between sips with his incredibly expressive lean fingers. But, as the evening wore on, the little maestro became more and more preoccupied. Suddenly he got up and rummaged through a suitcase, returning with a carefully folded

Mozart's Der Schauspieldirektor

letter which he handed around for the inspection of his companions. It was a letter he had carried with him for many years, written to him long ago when he was a sprouting young opera conductor in Italy. It was from the great Giuseppe Verdi. An old man's letter, it spoke encouragingly to the young conductor, telling him, among other things, to take good care of Verdi's operas in the long future that lay ahead of them. The musicians handed it around, poring over it with great respect. When they were finished, the maestro returned it to his valise. But he seemed even more troubled than before. Finally, with one of his characteristic little explosive grunts, he got what was troubling him out of his system. "An immortal," he remarked sadly. "Verdi will live forever. But Toscanini?" He gestured backward at his chin with one hand as if displaying himself as a detached object for their consideration. "Toscanini will be dead like all the rest. He will never conduct orchestras again. And the worst of it is" (here a fiery glint came into the little maestro's eye), "that they will play badly—badly!"

WINTHROP SARGEANT
Geniuses, Goddesses, and People, 1949

During his years at the helm of the Philadelphia Orchestra, Leopold Stokowski held complete mastery over that superb musical instrument. However, as the orchestra's biographer Herbert Kupferberg relates, Stokowski encountered much more difficulty taming the Philadelphia audience.

Stokowski was not only determined to remake the Philadelphia Orchestra; he also set out to reform the Philadelphia audience—which was, perhaps, an even more difficult task. His especial target was the Friday afternoon gathering. The ladies for the most part doted upon the blond young man, but they had no intention of letting him alter long-established habits which went back to the days of Scheel and Pohling. They sat and knitted while the music was being played. They kept their hats fixed firmly on their heads despite requests in the programs to remove them. They talked and coughed and rustled. Most irritating of all to the new conductor, they arrived late and left early, for when there was a conflict between the running time of a Brahms symphony and the Paoli local, the train always won out.

Soon after his triumph in the Mahler *Symphony of a Thousand* had securely established his place as the city's virtual musical dictator, Stokowski, armed with a new contract running through 1921 at an estimated salary of $40,000 a year, began to turn on his feminine audience, subjecting them to a torrent of words, some as acerbic and prickly as the modern music he was now playing in increasing amounts. Of course, they adored being admonished by him for their sins of deportment, and he relished lecturing, scolding, and chiding them. . . .

The battle over arrivals and departures went on for years, and was never really resolved. Although Stokowski did shame some of the worst offenders into quiescence, the afternoon outflux never quite stopped altogether. One famous Stokowski story tells of his being greeted by a female American tourist one summer in Rome. "I recall your face, madame," said Stokowski, "but I can't quite remember who you are." "I'm one of the old ladies with bundles," replied the tourist sweetly. Reminiscing about the old days, veteran concertgoer Mary C. Smith of Haverford, Pa., recalled her grandmother, Mrs. E. Wallace Matthews, stomping up a side-aisle during an early performance of Richard Strauss' *Death and Transfiguration*, calling back over her shoulder: "When *my* time comes, I hope there won't be so much brass."

Stokowski's war on latecomers reached its climax on a Friday afternoon in April, 1926, in an incident that not only had Philadelphia talking for weeks, but was reported widely throughout the United States. The program for that day was highly unusual. It opened with a very obscure work, a Fantasie by the late nineteenth-century Belgian conductor Guillaume Lekeu, and closed with Haydn's *Farewell* Symphony. Somewhere between was Wagner's *Ride of the Valkyries*.

This was, to put it mildly, an odd combination, but its significance became apparent quickly. The Lekeu work is written for small orchestra, with only the first violin and first cello playing at the start. These were the only two players actually on the stage when Stokowski mounted the podium and began to conduct, the others drifting in just before they were due to start playing. In fact, one or two had to start while they were still walking toward their seats, so tardy were they in arriving.

When the time came for the *Ride of the Valkyries* to begin, only the small band required for the Lekeu was on the stage; the rest of the players' seats were still empty. Nevertheless, Stokowski raised his baton preparing to give the downbeat. Before he could start, a group of brass players rushed in to take their seats. Then another breathless group arrived as the conductor again lowered his baton. After several more instrumentalists hastened into their seats the full complement was finally in place and the performance began. By now the audience realized that its own habitual tardiness was being mimicked, and there were some murmurings and a few hisses. The climax of the concert came in the *Farewell* Symphony in which, of course, the score calls for the players to depart individually until only the last two violinists remain to play the concluding measures—almost the reverse of the opening Lekeu work. Stokowski embellished the *Farewell* Symphony a bit, by having the players look at their watches and stir about impatiently just prior to their departure. At the end, as he faced an empty stage, Stokowski signalled to his phantom "orchestra" to take a bow, then turned around himself and bowed solemnly to the buzzing house.

While many in the audience accepted the ribbing in good humor, a considerable number of the matinee regulars were outraged by Stokowski's behavior. The next day management officials tried to explain

Brahms' Sonata for Two Pianos, Opus 34 B, F Minor

that the Lekeu and Haydn works had simply been played as written, with no insult to the audience intended. Later on, though, it became known that Stokowski had instructed the players to imitate the actions of the latecomers in the audience. In any case, he felt that he had made his point, and that particular experiment was not repeated.

Stokowski also took to haranguing his audiences whenever he felt they were coughing or sneezing too much during performances. Many women began arming themselves with cough drops on the way in, and one subscriber suggested to the management "that booths be installed at convenient locations in the Academy lobby on concert days for the sale of cough drops and soothing syrups of diverse kinds, after the manner of sale of opera books and librettos."

But cough drops, wherever bought, didn't seem to help much. Stokowski once bid the audience cease its "disagreeable and disgusting noises," and when a sneeze occurred during Gluck's *Alceste* Overture, followed by the arrival of several stragglers, he simply stopped playing and walked out. In the spring of 1927, when it was announced he was taking a six-month furlough to travel to the Far East, he bid farewell to his Friday matinee audience with this parting shot: "Goodby for a long time. I hope when I come back your colds will be all better."

HERBERT KUPFERBERG
Those Fabulous Philadelphians, 1969

Although the Boston Symphony has always been recognized as an out-standing orchestra, it reached a peak of perfection under the leadership of Serge Koussevitzky. Harry Ellis Dickson, a violinist with the Boston Symphony during the Koussevitzky era, wrote the following affectionate portrait of the maestro.

The history of the Boston Symphony Orchestra will forever be classified into two eras: B.K. (before Koussevitzky) and A.K. (after Koussevitzky). From the time he first came to the orchestra in 1924 through the twenty-five years of his conductorship he was able to establish and maintain an aura of Olympian aloofness and royal untouchability. His sartorial splendor, his beautiful carriage, his reserved but dramatic gestures on the podium, all of these endeared him immediately to the Back Bay ladies. Serge Koussevitzky was an actor, a sincere and wonderful actor who not only portrayed a role but actually lived it and passionately believed in that role. . . .

The question of Koussevitzky's musicianship has long been debated by critics, musicologists, and players and I leave the final judgment to posterity. I am convinced he was the greatest conductor who ever lived. Whether or not he was a deeply intellectual student of music, the fact is that he made music, that he felt it through every fiber of his being. It might be said that Koussevitzky approached music first with his heart, then with his mind. He had unfailing musical instincts and instinctive good taste in everything he did. Even when he was wrong he could, through his iron will and dynamic force, convince you that he was right. I have seen him argue with composers over their own music and, with rare exceptions, prevail. It was proven time and time again that Koussevitzky could present a composer's work infinitely better than the composer himself.

To him music could not exist without great beauty of sound and he is the only conductor I have ever known who spent hours of rehearsal time practicing sound. We would play certain passages over and over again "until," as he would say, "we will have 'our' sonority." One of his constant pleadings was for "more dolce." Indeed "dolce" became for him a word signifying perfection in music. If there was bad ensemble, he would shout, "Gentlemen, it is awfully not togedder! You must play more dolce." If he thought it was too loud, he would admonish the players to play more softly and "more dolce." If it was too soft, he would say, "I cannot hear the dolce." Not sustained enough? "Gentlemen, please don't made it a low in the music ... because when you made it a low the dolce was lost!" ...

The era of Koussevitzky was an exciting and turbulent one. Almost every rehearsal was a nightmare, every concert a thrilling experience. Those were the days when it was expected of conductors to be tyrannical and temperamental, and Koussevitzky was no exception. During his reign there were in the B.S.O. one hundred and five players and one hundred and six ulcers. (One man had two.)

But the concerts with Koussevitzky were wonderful. In spite of everything, he had a way of instilling into each musician a kind of pride and self-esteem that made him play better than his own capabilities. I don't remember a concert under Koussevitzky where, at the end, each player was not as soaking wet and emotionally spent as the conductor.

Koussevitzky had an intensively subjective approach to music, all kinds of music, it didn't matter what school, what style, what period. He simply loved music, and whatever he conducted he appropriated as his own, whether it was Tchaikovsky, Beethoven, or Bartók. Whenever he conducted a new work, whether or not he understood it, he would convince himself, and us, that this was the "greatest since Beethoven," and if the audience did not agree with him, he would walk off the stage muttering, "Idiot publicum!" and perhaps never play the piece again. His way with composers was imperious. "Aaron," he would say to Copland in the balcony while we were rehearsing a new work, "vy do you write mezzo-forte? You know mezzo-forte is di most baddest nuance *qui existe*. It must be pianissimo." And Copland would nod in agreement. With other composers he would have occasional difficulties. Hindemith, for example, would not let Koussey alter even one nuance.

Serge Koussevitzky was a born leader and he found it almost impossible to take orders from anybody, musical or otherwise. He was not a good accompanist for soloists, for unless things went his way they were

Schubert's Winterreise

apt not to go at all. I remember the Prokofiev G Minor Violin Concerto with Heifetz in which we finished a half bar after Heifetz, and there were others.

During the Koussevitzky era there were comparatively few soloists with the B.S.O. The glamour of Serge Koussevitzky was great enough to maintain full houses without soloists. And in all the eleven years I played under K. I do not remember an empty seat either in Symphony Hall or any of the other halls we played throughout the country. And such were the encomiums heaped upon him and the orchestra by critics and public that he would have had to be less than human not to have been influenced by it all. No wonder when a dear old lady said to him after a concert, "Doctor Koussevitzky, to us you are God," he answered "I know my responsibility!" There is also a story that after a concert a friend said, "You know, Serge Alexandrovitch, you are not only the greatest conductor, you are the *only* conductor!"

Koussey, pulling himself up, said, "Come now, there are other fine conductors in the world."

"Who?" asked the friend.

"Well . . ." And he turned to his wife: "Natasha, who?"

HARRY ELLIS DICKSON
"Gentlemen, More Dolce Please!" 1969

From 1939 until his death in 1971, Igor Stravinsky resided in the United States. Although much of his time and energy was spent on new compositions, Stravinsky also conducted concerts with many of the country's leading orchestras. On one such occasion in 1966, Stravinsky led the Houston Symphony Orchestra in a combined Bach-Stravinsky program. The novelist Paul Horgan, a close friend of the maestro and his wife, accompanied them to Houston and later wrote this intimate portrait of Stravinsky at work.

The hall manager received Stravinsky and led us backstage to a plaster-lined dressing room with metal make-up desk and a mirror, a black leatherette sofa, a chair, and a small bathroom. Stravinsky asked me to give over the scores to the manager who left to place them on the conductor's stand.

"How do you feel, Maestro?"

"For the moment, that is a needless question. Ask me after the rehearsal. I will now get ready—" this politely dismissive.

"I will be out front if you need me."

"Thank you," with a little bow.

I went to the auditorium. The orchestra under the work lights tuned and retuned their instruments, playing the Shah of Persia's music. . . . There was an invigorating air of tension over the stage, waiting for Stravinsky. Many looks were directed at the stage side from which he would enter. The Persian cacophony continued and then as suddenly as though a baton had wiped it out, it ceased, as Stravinsky, hobbling as little as possible with his stick, wearing a grey cardigan, with a towel folded about his neck like an ascot tie, and his left arm aloft in almost a Papal gesture of benediction and greeting, appeared in the harsh and stimulating light of a symphony rehearsal. The players rose and applauded. He made his way to the central stand, faced them, and bowed deeply to left, to center, and to right. His rehearsal etiquette was thus immediately established, to the visible pleasure of the orchestra. Then promptly to work.

In an habitual gesture, he licked the thumb and first finger of his left hand and turned the cover of the score on his desk. In a lifted voice, colored by comradely humor, he said, making a pun on the title of the Bach chorale,

"Ladies and gentlemen, we will begin by coming down from heaven to earth."

There was a ripple of appreciative amusement over the stage, and then, abruptly serious, he spread his arms, his strong square hands furled for the up-down beat, he created the new sort of silence required of the moment, and then broke it clearly and gravely.

His rehearsal manners were an effective mixture of strict professionalism and sympathetic courtesy. He was vigorous in his beat and in his cues, and he swiftly alternated his gaze from the pages of his score and the players. There was never in his conducting a flourish for its own sake. His score-indications had of course long been familiar to him and he built his fabric of sound out of the original auditory concept. His better-known works had for decades acquired a sort of "public" sound —that patina of temperament overlaid upon them by the versions of different conductors in recordings and in concerts. All such was swept away when he conducted his own works, and the result was that their anatomy emerged in their primal purity. Total logic was what he sought, never the momentary fragmental effect. . . .

In the morning [the following Monday] there was another rehearsal, much like those of Saturday and Sunday. Monday afternoon was given over to rest before the first concert. . . . The day seemed at moments to approach the evening concert with unsettling swiftness, and at others, to drag along at an exasperating and ominous pace, both conditions producing hollow nervousness even in myself, who had but to carry scores and extra towels, and a small bag containing perhaps an extra shirt, and, surely, assorted medicaments whose presence in the dressing room would be a comfort, even should no dosages be required.

The management had provided a box for Madame [Mrs. Stravinsky], Mirandi [Levy, a family friend], and myself. I went backstage with Stravinsky while Madame and Mirandi remained in the auditorium. He was somewhat abstracted, his concentration already forming for the work ahead. His movements as he adjusted his professional possessions on the make-up counter, his neatness in all things, were executed as slowly as in a dream. It was no time for small talk, but tension

Boccherini's Opera 42

is contagious, and I relieved mine by remarking on the fine cut and fit of his tailcoat.

"Thirty-five years ago or more," he said, smiling broadly. "I had it made in London"—the same tailcoat, surely!

He wore a soft white shirt with collar turned down, and a white tie. Dimly away was the sound of the orchestra already on the stage, tuning and riffling.

"Pol," he said, "please, come back in the intermission to keep the door. Not to see anyone during the intermission." . . .

His workmanlike rehearsals had produced excellent results. The Bach variations proceeded in the stately balance he had labored for, and the ceremony between orchestra and chorus was beautiful to see as well as hear. The meeting of two masters in the work was a lesson out of *The Poetics of Music*, when in our very presence, we heard how "tradition . . . appears as an heirloom, a heritage that one receives before passing it on to one's descendants," for if Bach was there, so, too, and unmistakably, was Stravinsky.

He left the stage and it seemed to us he was gone a fairly long time, and Madame gave me an inquiring look. I was about to go to the dressing room for news when he reappeared, and it later turned out that he had needed to rearrange his hernia appliance, which had slipped—a tedious process, as it meant undressing and dressing almost entirely. But when he lifted his arm for *Orpheus*, his power was all present, and for the duration of that score I was concerned with nothing but the work itself.

He received so many calls that I was in the dressing room for many minutes before he returned. He came in, seized a towel, and began patting his face with it, while in pantomime he instructed me to lock the door. White with perspiration, he was catching his breath in long draughts through his nose. His little chest rose and fell like the top half of a pair of bellows. I believed he should lie down. I offered him a fresh towel which he took. Someone knocked and I opened the door a slit and said that Maestro Stravinsky asked to be excused from seeing anyone, and then I locked us in again. He was rapidly coming down to ordinary respiration and I suppose heartbeat. I felt it suitable to say, now,

"Well, Maestro, when I hear you conduct, I feel that not only do most conductors do things that are quite unnecessary, but are often actually harmful."

He threw down the towel. He took my shoulders and declared in a voice of high glee,

"Pol! I h-h-ate interpretation!"

I delighted in his vehemence. I laughed—I had not before heard him actually state this famous position. In the context of that dressing room, I could not fail to have a fleeting thought of its absent resident.

"The concert is wonderful," I said, "and the *Orpheus*!"

He had no need to hear superlatives from me, but he saw my excitement, and pulling me to the dressing table where duplicates of the evening's scores lay, he opened to certain pages of *Orpheus*, and began to explain to me the musical anatomy of certain passages. This inversion. That progression. Variation of a phrase prominently heard earlier in a different scoring. To the grasp of these abstract niceties I was inadequate but this did not lessen my fascination with the fact of his demonstration. His animation was as fresh as if the work had just been composed, and despite my inadequacy in technical matters, I received a direct and powerful demonstration of the primacy of form among all the elements of creation in any art. At the same time, in my hinterthought, I was nagged by other questions—the couch; a quick shower or sponging; a fresh shirt; at least attention to the 'ernia and its retainer. But before there was time for anything else, even for finishing the elucidation of the *Orpheus* score, there was a tap at the door, and the call boy said, "Ready, Mr. Stravinsky, please," and the intermission was spent. It had been spent for me, for my interest, in response to my great elation at the performance.

"Is there anything I may do for you before I go out front again?"

"No, thank you, my de-ar," he said, "but come back immediately, we will all escape."

And so we did, after a performance of *L'Oiseau de feu* which rose to a thundering climax more theatrical and audience-rousing than I had ever heard, all despite strict canons of taste against "interpretation." Stokowski could not have produced a more overpowering crescendo than that with which the composer himself closed the piece. Houston leaped to its feet, and later, backstage, crowded the cement corridors; but with self-accusing charm, Stravinsky, wearing a great fur coat (sables? martens?) like the one which had belonged to his father, the pre-Chaliapin Imperial Opera basso, made his way past hands which pulled at him, and the voices of patronesses hoping to halt him with fascinating anecdotes—"heard you conduct in Paris in 1922"—"met you and your charming wife on the *Ile de France* and we all had a drink together"—"Ah just cain't stay away tomorrow naght, Ah'm comin' again, mystro"—and we at last were encapsulated in the limousine and on our way to the Rice Hotel, and early bed. Nothing much was said in the car. Stravinsky descended into stillness and I felt that some dissatisfaction was at work in him. He would have supper sent up by room service. As we parted he politely said goodnight.

PAUL HORGAN
Encounter with Stravinsky, 1972

Handel's Messiah

In the first volume of Arthur Rubinstein's autobiography, My Younger Years, *he narrates the story of his initial concert appearance in the United States, in 1906, and the storm touched off by an innocent breach of orchestral protocol.*

Anxious to see what the tuner had done to my piano, I arrived at Carnegie Hall half an hour before rehearsal time, but I found many of the

orchestra's musicians already on the stage enjoying the familiar cacophony of tuning and trying out their respective instruments. At ten sharp, the conductor, Mr. Fritz Scheel, appeared and, without losing a second, began to rehearse the overture of Weber which was to precede my concerto.

Scheel was the typical German musician, well trained, solid, but cold. The orchestra played splendidly—it would have been a dream, I thought, to hear it under a Nikisch! When my turn came, Mr. Scheel asked me right away, "Are you related to the 'great' Rubenstein?" [The Russian pianist Anton Rubenstein] I had heard this question often before, but it irritated me this time more than ever. The piano sounded better, to my great relief; the tuner had kept his promise, so I played my long solo introduction to the concerto better than I had feared I would; after a few minutes I had the orchestra on my side. The rehearsal went very well. Mr. Scheel was efficient and indifferent, though my dynamic tempo in the last movement did stir up some reaction in him. I returned to the hotel in good spirits and spent the rest of the day in anticipation. In the evening, well ahead of time, Mr. Ulrich came to take me to the concert.

"The hall is well filled," he said with satisfaction, "and William Knabe and his brother Ernest [piano manufacturers] and their wives have arrived from Baltimore and invite you for supper after the concert." I had sat barely twenty minutes in the artists' room—the overture was short—when they called me to go up on the stage. The well-lit hall, filled with people, looked twice as big as in the morning. My appearance was greeted with a warm applause. As I made my bows I became aware of a gift which served me well through my entire concert career: the bigger the hall, the larger the audience, the more confidence and self-control I felt, and I had none of the paralyzing stage fright which afflicts so many of the best concert performers. And so I attacked my concerto with a tremendous impact. The public applauded each movement, and at the end of the brilliant finale I received a roaring ovation. I brought the conductor out, twice, to acknowledge the applause, and shook hands with the concertmaster, but the public would not give up and shouted "Bravo," and "More, more," called me back three or four times, and finally forced me to give an encore. I played the A flat Polonaise of Chopin with pride. The ovation doubled, and I had to add another piece before they calmed down. An anticlimax awaited me in the artists' room. "How dare you give encores!" Fritz Scheel screamed at me, foaming with rage. "You ruined my concert—I won't let you play again with my orchestra"; and he left the room, slamming the door behind him.

I was speechless. I hadn't known that encores were taboo at symphony concerts; in Europe they were generally accepted. Scheel's threat was a great blow; it killed the joy of my success. Suddenly the door opened, and a real crowd entered the room. Mr. Ulrich, beaming, shook my hand as if it were a pump, slapped me on the back, and shouted, "Great, you were great, you made it!" Then he introduced me to the two members of the Knabe family, who were very nice, and their wives; the two men gave me a hug, their wives kissed me. William, the elder brother, said cheerfully, "Take your time. After you have had a rest, we will take you to a good supper." At that moment Armand [a young French count and friend of Rubinstein's] appeared, followed by some friends whom he introduced to me. I, in turn, introduced him to the Knabes. His title, as usual produced a magic effect. They babbled, "Will you do us the honor and join us at supper, count?" "Count, this is a real pleasure." It was as if they were trying to learn how to pronounce "Count," they used it so often. Armand, courteous as ever, kissed the hands of the ladies and accepted the invitation. He was determined anyway to spend the evening with me.

When I told Mr. Knabe and Mr. Ulrich about Mr. Scheel's outburst, they were indignant. "He is obliged to continue the concerts with you," said Mr. Knabe. "We paid for it." Vastly relieved, I started to sign cheerfully some autographs for the waiting crowd, while my party waited patiently. Finally we were able to leave. Three hansoms, the English-styled two-wheeled cabs, took us to Delmonico's, one of the two most fashionable supper places in New York then. ... The place was packed, but the Knabes had a table reserved. Both brothers were in their early thirties, tall and rather good-looking; their wives were young and pretty. And the four of them were gay! My success was toasted at every drink, but "the Count" remained the center of their attention. They invited him to come to their home town of Baltimore, where I had my next concert, and Armand promised to come. I was well pleased with my debut in America. The critics, next morning, expressed divided opinions about my performance; two reviews were enthusiastic, one augured a great future for me, another one praised my technique and brilliance but thought less of my musicianship, and one critic, a Mr. Krehbiel, did not like me at all. ...

I seemed to be characterized as "a great talent, a fine temperament, the promise of a brilliant career, but still immature ... he has much to learn." I must admit that this was also my own opinion.

ARTHUR RUBINSTEIN
My Younger Years, 1973

Paris in the early twentieth century was no less a center for musical activity than it was for art and writing. Of the many American composers who lived and studied in Paris, the vast majority received instruction in harmony and composition from a remarkable Frenchwoman, Nadia Boulanger. Aaron Copland, one of Mlle. Boulanger's most renowned pupils, recalls the qualities which made her such a brilliant mentor.

It is almost forty years since first I rang the bell at Nadia Boulanger's Paris apartment and asked her to accept me as her composition pupil.

Chopin's Polonaise, Opus 26, No. 1

Any young musician may do the same thing today, for Mademoiselle Boulanger lives at the same address in the same apartment and teaches with the same formidable energy. The only difference is that she was then comparatively little known outside the Paris music world and today there are few musicians anywhere who would not concede her to be the most famous of living composition teachers.

Our initial meeting had taken place in the Palace of Fontainebleau several months before that first Paris visit. Through the initiative of Walter Damrosch a summer music school for American students was established in a wing of the palace in 1921 and Nadia Boulanger was on the staff as teacher of harmony. I arrived, fresh out of Brooklyn, aged twenty, and all agog at the prospect of studying composition in the country that had produced Debussy and Ravel. A fellow-student told me about Mademoiselle Boulanger and convinced me that a look-in on her harmony class would be worth my while. I needed convincing—after all, I had already completed my harmonic studies in New York and couldn't see how a harmony teacher could be of any help to me. What I had not foreseen was the power of Mademoiselle Boulanger's personality and the special glow that informs her every discussion of music whether on the simplest or the most exalted plane.

The teaching of harmony is one thing; the teaching of advanced composition is something else again. The reason they differ so much is that harmonic procedures are deduced from known common practice while free composition implies a subtle mixing of knowledge and instinct for the purpose of guiding the young composer toward a goal that can only be dimly perceived by both student and teacher. Béla Bartók used to claim that teaching composition was impossible to do well; he himself would have no truck with it. Mademoiselle Boulanger would undoubtedly agree that it is difficult to do well—and then go right on trying.

Actually Nadia Boulanger was quite aware that as a composition teacher she labored under two further disadvantages: she was not herself a regularly practicing composer and in so far as she composed at all she must of necessity be listed in that unenviable category of the woman composer. . . .

It would be easy to sketch a portrait of Mademoiselle Boulanger as a personality in her own right. Those who meet her or hear her talk are unlikely to forget her physical presence. Of medium height and pleasant features, she gave off, even as a young woman, a kind of objective warmth. She had none of the ascetic intensity of a Martha Graham or the toughness of a Gertrude Stein. On the contrary, in those early days she possessed an almost old-fashioned womanliness—a womanliness that seemed quite unaware of its own charm. Her low-heeled shoes and long black skirts and pince-nez glasses contrasted strangely with her bright intelligence and lively temperament. In more recent years she has become smaller and thinner. . . . But her low-pitched voice is as resonant as ever and her manner has lost none of its decisiveness. . . .

As her reputation spread, students came to her not only from America but also from Turkey, Poland, Chile, Japan, England, Norway, and many other countries. How, I wonder, would each of them describe what Mademoiselle gave him as teacher? How indeed does anyone describe adequately what is learned from a powerful teacher? I myself have never read a convincing account of the progress from student stage to that of creative maturity through a teacher's ministrations. And yet it happens: some kind of magic does indubitably rub off on the pupil. It begins, perhaps, with the conviction that one is in the presence of an exceptional musical mentality. By a process of osmosis one soaks up attitudes, principles, reflections, knowledge. That last is a key word: it is literally exhilarating to be with a teacher for whom the art one loves has no secrets.

Nadia Boulanger knew everything there was to know about music; she knew the oldest and the latest music, pre-Bach and post-Stravinsky, and knew it cold. All technical know-how was at her fingertips: harmonic transposition, the figured bass, score reading, organ registration, instrumental techniques, structural analyses, the school fugue and the free fugue, the Greek modes and Gregorian chant. Needless to say this list is far from exhaustive. She was particularly intrigued by new musical developments. I can still remember the eagerness of her curiosity concerning my jazz-derived rhythms of the early twenties, a corner of music that had somehow escaped her. Before long we were exploring polyrhythmic devices together—their cross-pulsations, their notations, and especially their difficulty of execution intrigued her. This was typical, nothing under the heading of music could possibly be thought of as foreign. I am not saying that she liked or even approved of all kinds of musical expression—far from it. But she had the teacher's consuming need to know how all music functions, and it was that kind of inquiring attitude that registered on the minds of her students.

More important to the budding composer than Mademoiselle Boulanger's technical knowledge was her way of surrounding him with an air of confidence. (The reverse—her disapproval, I am told, was annihilating in its effect.) In my own case she was able to extract from a composer of two-page songs and three-page piano pieces a full-sized ballet lasting thirty-five minutes. True, no one has ever offered to perform the completed ballet, but the composing of it proved her point—I was capable of more than I myself thought possible. This mark of confidence was again demonstrated when, at the end of my three years of study, Mademoiselle Boulanger asked me to write an organ concerto for her first American tour, knowing full well that I had only a nodding acquaintance with the king of instruments and that I had never heard a note of my own orchestration. "Do you really think I can do it?" I asked hopefully. "*Mais oui*" was the firm reply—and so I did.

Mademoiselle gave the world première of the work—a Symphony for organ and orchestra—on January 11, 1925, under the baton of Walter Damrosch. My parents, beaming, sat with me in a box. Imagine

Gluck's Orfeo

our surprise when the conductor, just before beginning the next work on the program, turned to his audience and said: "If a young man, at the age of twenty-three, can write a symphony like that, in five years he will be ready to commit murder!" The asperities of my harmonies had been too much for the conductor, who felt that his faithful subscribers needed reassurance that he was on their side. Mademoiselle Boulanger, however, was not to be swayed; despite her affection for Mr. Damrosch she wavered not in the slightest degree in her favorable estimate of my symphony. . . .

Many of these observations are based, of course, on experiences of a good many years ago. Much has happened to music since that time. The last decade, in particular, cannot have been an easy time for the teacher of composition, and especially for any teacher of the older generation. The youngest composers have taken to worshiping at strange shrines. . . .

In the meantime it must be a cause for profound satisfaction to Mademoiselle Boulanger that she has guided the musical destiny of so many gifted musicians: Igor Markevitch, Jean Françaix, and Marcelle de Manziarly in France; Americans like Walter Piston, Virgil Thomson, Roy Harris, Marc Blitzstein, among the older men, Elliott Carter, David Diamond, Irving Fine, Harold Shapero, Arthur Berger among the middle generation, and youngsters like Easley Blackwood during the fifties.

In 1959, when Harvard University conferred an honorary degree on Nadia Boulanger, a modest gesture was made toward recognition of her standing as teacher and musician. America, unfortunately, has no reward commensurate with what Nadia Boulanger has contributed to our musical development. But, in the end, the only reward she would want is the one she already has: the deep affection of her many pupils everywhere.

AARON COPLAND
Copland on Music, 1960

Marian Anderson's 1939 Easter Sunday concert in front of the Lincoln Memorial was a truly unprecedented musical event. As Miss Anderson's manager, Sol Hurok was involved in every aspect of the planning and execution of the concert. Hurok's description of those activities, as told in Impresario, *the first volume of his memoirs, gives a firsthand glimpse of Miss Anderson's artistry and grace under extreme pressure.*

The *cause célèbre* which came to its climax at the Lincoln Memorial on Easter Sunday in 1939 began with a perfectly routine request from Howard University in Washington, D.C., for a concert by Marian Anderson under the University's auspices. Arrangements were made in June, 1938, for a concert to take place in Washington the next season.

When we were scheduling Marian's tour the date we gave the University was April 9th.

Early in January, 1939, the manager of Howard University's concert series applied to Fred E. Hand, manager of Constitution Hall, to reserve the auditorium for a performance on April 9th. . . .

Mr. Hand replied to the University's manager that a clause in the rental contract of Constitution Hall prohibits the presentation of Negro artists. . . .

When the University informed us of the clause, we wrote to Mr. Hand, asking him if it would be possible to waive the restriction in the case of Miss Anderson, so as not to deny to the people of Washington a great musical experience.

Back came the reply from Mr. Hand: "I beg to advise you that Constitution Hall is not available on April 9th, 1939, because of prior commitments." In the matter of policy, he advised us to communicate with Mrs. Henry M. Robert, Jr., President General of the National Society, Daughters of the American Revolution. . . .

Marks Levine, my good friend, of National Concert and Artists Corporation, wrote to Mr. Hand at about this time asking for available dates for a concert by Ignaz Paderewski in Constitution Hall. Hand replied with a list of dates which did not include the 9th, but did mention the 8th and 10th as open. I wired the University's concert manager that the 8th and 10th were open and he promptly applied to Hand for either date.

The answer came back: "The Hall is not available for a concert by Miss Anderson."

Now the facts were clear. The 9th might very well be closed, but neither was any other date open to Marian Anderson at Constitution Hall. Indignation began to sizzle. . . .

Protesting telegrams continued to pour into the office of the DAR. Newspaper editorial pages bristled with editorials, crackled with letters to the editors.

And on February 27th Mrs. Roosevelt resigned from the DAR. . . .

On February 24th I had announced that Marian Anderson would sing in Washington, out of doors, within earshot of the Daughters and their Hall. I sent my press agent, Gerry Goode, to Washington with the intention of asking permission to use the Lincoln Memorial for the concert.

Walter White, the sparkplug president of the NAACP, was on his way to Washington too. Together they went to the Department of Interior, which has jurisdiction over the parks of the capital. Assistant Secretary Oscar L. Chapman listened, nodded, said, "Wait a minute," went into Secretary Ickes' office, and came back. In literally one minute the Secretary had granted permission for Miss Anderson to sing a concert at the Lincoln Memorial. . . .

Platform, public-address system, ropes to mark the aisles—all had to be provided. And the complicated business of the radio network, news-

Beethoven's Trio for Piano and Strings, Opus 70, No. 1, D Major

reel cameras, sound-recording devices had to be handled by an expert. My publicity staff was on hand to give the radio, newsreel and newspaper men the service they have come to expect in this highly organized modern world. . . .

We gave our services, we paid the incidental expenses, but this is one event I do not claim as a publicity stunt. Anyone who has read the record knows it was as nearly spontaneous an arising of men and women of good will in Washington as there can be in our times. Well managed, of course. No untoward events. No jarring notes.

Easter Sunday came closer. All the arrangements were made. Everything was ready. For us the excitement mounted until it was almost unbearable.

And on Saturday, at about midnight, Marian telephoned from Philadelphia, "Must we really go through with this?"

For Marian it had been a difficult time. The denial of the Hall . . . was a painful shock to begin with. And then the storm of protest that swirled about her innocent head, welcome as it was for the sake of principle, violated all her personal needs for privacy, serenity, peace. I have said it before and it bears repeating: Marian has not the instincts nor the temperament of a fighter. And when, through no fault of hers, the issue arose and the fight was on, she was as uncomfortable as one might well be at the center of a cyclone. Willingly as she did her part in the service of her people, she would far rather it had been some other, someone who could enjoy the fight.

And so on the eve of her greatest concert she telephoned in a state of actual fright to ask whether we really had to go through with it.

But when we took her from Union Station to Governor Pinchot's house, with the sirens of a police escort shrieking through the quiet Sunday-morning streets, she was calm and ready. At the Governor's, she changed to her concert gown and quietly glanced over her music once more, while the police captain stood on the sidewalk nervously counting the seconds ticking by. We drove to the Lincoln Memorial in a trance of hushed expectancy. As she walked beside me along the roped-off aisle and up the steps to the platform, where great men and women of America stood to honor her, the arm which I took to steady her was steadier than my own. She raised her eyes once to the great bronze figure with so much sorrow in the deeply lined face. Then she turned to the people who had come to hear her and to pledge by their presence there a faith in the rights of man.

There were 75,000 of them. To describe a crowd of 75,000 men and women—and children, too—standing with upturned faces, expectant, quiet, attentive, is beyond my powers. The effect of such a mass of human beings, their eyes and ears and very hearts fixed on one figure, is indescribable. Looking down at them, one feels a kind of buoyancy, as though one were floating on a sea—and it was a sea, with a tide of strong feeling flowing from them to the erect figure of a woman standing composed and ready by the piano on the platform.

When she opened her lips and sang, it was as though the tide flowed back again to them. She returned to them, with all the sincerity in her, the human goodness which they had offered her. We have come to expect of Marian and her singing not only the beautiful instrument beautifully used, but the truly great power of music. We listen, not only to be sung to, but to be exalted. On that Easter Sunday 75,000 Americans shared in that exaltation, and it shone in their faces.

A mural painting of that Easter Sunday afternoon, the work of Mitchell Jamieson, adorns a wall in the Department of Interior building. At the dedication in January, 1943, Secretary Ickes said, "Her voice and personality have come to be a symbol—a symbol of the willing acceptance of the immortal truth that 'all men are created free and equal.'"

To which Marian replied, "I am deeply touched that I can be in any way a symbol of democracy. Everyone present was a living witness to the ideals of freedom for which President Lincoln died. When I sang that day I was singing to the entire Nation."

SOL HUROK
Impresario, 1946

Wagner's Das Rheingold

The annual outdoor summer concerts at Lewisohn Stadium on the campus of the City College of New York were an integral part of New York's cultural landscape for more than four decades until they were suspended in 1966. Responsibility for hiring artists, arranging schedules, raising funds, and checking the weather forecasts fell to Minnie Guggenheimer, a diminutive woman whose energy and good humor became a hallmark of the series. From a place at her mother's side, Sophie Untermeyer shared those exciting evenings at Lewisohn Stadium, as she describes in the following excerpts from Mother is Minnie.

It has been estimated that almost as many people trek up to New York's Lewisohn Stadium on clear summer nights to chuckle over the intermission antics of Minnie Guggenheimer as to hear any of the world-famous singers, instrumental virtuosi and conductors she lines up for appearances with the Stadium Symphony Orchestra in her full-time, unsalaried job as impresaria of the world's largest-scale musical project.

Minnie's perennial tussles with such tongue twisters as Khatchaturian and Slenczynska over the Stadium loudspeakers; her persistent public confusion as to whether Moiseiwitsch is a ballet dancer, Szigeti plays the piano, or Beethoven wrote the Verdi *Requiem*; the unabashed bloopers and blithe malapropisms she perpetrates while rattling off advance programs and introducing celebrity guests; and the utter lack of inhibition with which she shares intimate household secrets and problems of dress and digestion with crowds running into the tens of thousands have become . . . a part of the New York legend. . . .

A short, busty, gray-haired dowager who might have stepped right out of a Helen Hokinson cartoon, Minnie will float from the wings of the vast outdoor stage at around 9:30 of a June or July night—in all likelihood wearing the same heavy, rubber-soled sport shoes and dowdy, five-year-old cotton dress she put on to walk the dog before breakfast, with a frumpy inverted flowerpot of a hat borrowed at the last minute from the cook—and, waving her right hand giddily in mid-air, chirp a cheery "Hello, everybody" to a motley mass that choruses its reciprocal "Hello, Minnie" in ecstatic unison. Then, planting herself behind a standing microphone and sliding her framed spectacles down the not inconsiderable length of her nose, she'll proceed to forecast the musical highlights of the week, identifying *Richard* Strauss as the composer of "The Beautiful Blue Danube" and *Pinafore* as everybody's favorite by Gilbert and *Solomon*; promising that *Anton* Rubinstein will play the Tchai-COW-sky *Violin* Con-SERT-o, Jan Peerce will sing the role of *Aida*, and *Rodger Hammerstein* "personally" will conduct a number from *South Pacific;* and interrupting herself from time to time to implore the echo of her own voice to "shut up" or exhort her listeners to "Tell everybody you know to come to the Stadium. And tell everybody you don't know too, because unless we have people in the empty seats I'll simply go bust!"

Habitual Stadiumgoers recall with particular delight the night in 1947 when she came out to herald the upcoming appearance of "one of the best-known names in the musical world," then, hesitating for an anguished moment, reached into her overstuffed pocketbook for the crumpled bank check on which she had written her notes and identified him as Ezio Pinza, *baass.*" "Oh dear, that can't be right," she corrected aloud. "A bass is a kind of fish!"...

Surviving two wars, a national depression, and an endless succession of local crises, the Stadium Concerts have provided for those of us who grew up in New York in the 1920's, '30s, '40s, and '50s an endless chain of memories, of works first heard, of personalities first experienced, of evenings under the spell of stars and great music. The long and notable line of Stadium soloists has run the gamut from Rosa Ponselle and Kirsten Flagstad to Frank Sinatra and Harry Belafonte; from Fritz Kreisler and Arthur Rubinstein to Benny Goodman and Errol Garner. The roster of conductors has ranged all the way from Beecham, Mitropoulos, Reiner, and Stokowski to Paul Whiteman and Duke Ellington. Victor Herbert and Sigmund Romberg, Villa-Lobos and Leonard Bernstein, Robert Stolz and Richard Rodgers have conducted their own works at the Stadium. Alicia Markova, Argentinita, and José Greco have danced across the big stage; Carl Sandburg has recited his poetry and Ethel Barrymore Colt read Shakespeare; Larry Adler and John Sebastian have played Bach and Mozart on the harmonica, and Léon Thérémin and Lucie Rosen have plucked eeire notes from the summer air with the aid of the mysterious instrument bearing Thérémin's name.

The average member of the audience for New York's famous summer symphonic programs, according to the results of a questionnaire circulated in 1952, attends the concerts regularly for at least twelve years of his life, going at least ten times a season. Although his own musical talent and training is limited to "a little piano," he has pretty definite ideas about the kind of music he likes to hear. His favorite symphony is the Beethoven Fifth; his favorite violin concerto the Beethoven "Emperor"; his favorite opera *Carmen;* his favorite song "Kiss Me Again" . . . and his favorite soloist Jascha Heifetz (with Lily Pons in second place and Arthur Rubinstein, Yehudi Menuhin, and Nathan Milstein close runners-up). . . .

The habitual Stadiumgoer likes to think of himself as a member of a large, yet fairly close-knit family, which shares with favorite public figures their intimate problems and personal joys and sorrows. . . . He was proud that night in 1942 when a fine young pianist was given time off from the army to play at the Stadium and Captain Sam Russell came onstage at intermission to promote Private Eugene List to the rank of corporal. He suppressed a tear or two when plucky Marjorie Lawrence was rolled out in a wheel chair to sing Brünnhilde's "Immolation" in one of her first public appearances after a crippling attack of polio. He welcomed the news that lovely Roberta Peters and handsome Robert Merrill, just married in a wedding ceremony of fairy-tale splendor, would be returning from their honeymoon for a joint concert at the Stadium; then wondered what strange feelings the young baritone must have had facing his wife of only a few weeks, wearing her wedding dress onstage a day after their divorce had been made public. He shouted "bravo" for Arthur Schuller, a second violinist in the Stadium orchestra, directing his fellow players for the first time in a valiant eleventh-hour pinch hit, while holding a little silent prayer for the scheduled conductor, Miguel Sandoval, who had keeled over on the podium rehearsing the same program earlier in the day and was gasping for the last breaths of a brilliantly gifted life in a hospital a few blocks away. And if he happens to be one of the hepcats whom new concepts of programming have lured to the Stadium in increasing numbers in recent seasons, he is not likely to forget that dramatic moment, midway through the 1959 July Fourth "Jazz Jamboree," when a grand old showman who had been reported fatally ill only a week before in Italy and for whom five or six top bandleaders had volunteered at the last minute to substitute, wandered out from the wings virtually unnoticed, flashed a familiar grin to his "All-Stars," snatched a trumpet from one of them and gave forth with the first blaring reassurance that Louis Armstrong was in the groove again, while thousands burst exuberantly into "Happy Birthday, dear Satchmo" on the fifty-ninth anniversary of his coming into the world in a dismal New Orleans back alley.

Throughout Stadium Concerts' history there have been moments of thrilling new discovery to treasure. Perhaps the night in 1930 when a dance program starring Anna Duncan, adopted daughter of the illus-

Verdi's Ernani

trious Isadora, provided a red-headed young fiddler from the Capitol Theatre Orchestra with his first chance to wield a symphonic baton. Said the music critic of the New York *World* the next day: "His technique, sharp and incisive and peculiarly toneless, is better suited to the theater." But the Stadium audience disagreed vociferously, as have audiences (and more astute critics) all around the world in the ensuing years, hailing Eugene Ormandy as one of the giants of the podium. . . .

They still speak with special affection of a night in 1925 when a nervous young contralto no one had ever heard of till then stepped timidly before the orchestra to sing "O Mio Fernando" from Donizetti's *La Favorita* and brought the house down with her breath-taking trill at the end of the aria. She had been given her first big-time engagement as winner over three hundred and sixty contestants in a series of talent auditions held throughout the previous winter on behalf of Stadium Concerts. At a table way up in front near the stage, the work-hardened hands of Anna Anderson, a Negro laundress from Philadelphia, applauded with special pride for her daughter Marian.

On July 25, 1927, a twenty-nine-year-old composer from Brooklyn, with a number of successful Broadway show scores to his credit, was to appear for the first time at the Stadium, providing another unforgettable experience as he played his own jazz-infused piano concerto and a haunting utterance of twentieth century frustration called *Rhapsody in Blue* with the orchestra under the baton of Willem Van Hoogstraten. He made a tremendous hit with the audience and reappeared as piano soloist on varied symphonic programs in each of the four succeeding years. Then in 1932 a rush of seventeen thousand eight hundred and forty-five of his fans through the turnstiles broke all previous Stadium attendance records for the first of the memorable All-Gershwin concerts, with William Daley and Albert Coates sharing the podium, Gershwin playing the *Rhapsody in Blue* himself, and his virtually unknown young friend Oscar Levant playing the Piano Concerto. Five years later, George Gershwin, only thirty-nine, was dead in Hollywood of a brain tumor, and a vast audience, saddened by the loss of one of America's most promising musical talents, paid tribute to his memory at the Stadium. . . .

Sophie G. Untermeyer
Mother Is Minnie, 1960

During the 1930's the jazz-derived big band sound known as "swing" dominated popular music. Bands lead by Benny Goodman, Tommy and Jimmy Dorsey, and Woody Herman traveled across the country, appearing in hotels and nightclubs as well as on radio broadcasts and college campuses. Nevertheless, as Benny Goodman wrote in an informal history of this era, The Kingdom of Swing, *no one expected the frenzied adulation that greeted his band on the opening day of an appearance at the Paramount Theatre in New York City.*

By the time we finished our job in "The Big Broadcast of 1937," which was made in the summer of *1936*, we had a pretty good idea that the public for real jazz was a big one, and growing all the time. Even when we opened at the Pennsylvania, some of the people around the hotel were skeptical, saying the band was too loud. That was a big night for me. . . . After the band was set in the room and the crowds started to come and keep on coming, we didn't hear much more comment on the band being loud. But I don't think that any of us realized how strong a hold it had on the youngsters until a certain day early in March 1937.

We had undertaken to double at the Paramount Theatre in New York in addition to playing our job at the Pennsylvania, with no expectation that we would do more than fair business. After all, our only previous theater bookings had been something less than sensational. So when we arrived at the theater for an early morning rehearsal before the first show and found a couple of hundred kids lined up in front of the box-office at about 7 A.M., we couldn't help feeling that every one of our most loyal supporters in the five boroughs was already on hand.

However, this wasn't a patch on what happened even before we got on stage. All through the showing of the picture, the folks backstage said there were noises and whistling coming through from the house as Claudette Colbert did her stuff in "Maid of Salem." The theater was completely full an hour before we were supposed to go on, and when we finally came up on the rising platform, the noise sounded like Times Square on New Year's Eve. It certainly was a lot different from the days when I played on that same platform with Eddie Paul's orchestra.

The crowd quieted down a little when the band started in, but even on stage you could get an undercurrent of intense excitement that really did something to us. That reception topped anything we had known up to that time, and because we felt it was spontaneous and genuine, we got a tremendous kick out of it. It's only in these latter days, when some of the youngsters just come to cut up that it gets in our way. After all, if a fellow like Jess Stacy or Ziggy Elman or Vernon Brown gets up to play a solo, he has a right to be heard—and the people in the audience who know what they're listening to feel the same way about it.

However, we didn't know half the story until we got off the stage and were back in our dressing rooms. It seems that Willard was sitting in the mezzanine with Bob Weitman, the manager of the Paramount. They got the same thrill out of this enthusiasm that we did, up to the point where a couple of youngsters got up and started to shag in the aisles. Then a few more started to climb over the rail towards the orchestra, and Bob jumped up and rushed out, yelling:

"Somebody's going to get hurt there any minute. There'll be a panic."

He ran down the steps to the back of the orchestra, and as soon as the ushers saw him, they snapped to attention and started saluting.

"The hell with that," he shouted. "Get down there and stop those kids from killing themselves!"

As he went from aisle to aisle to get the ushers organized, he had to go through this same routine of being saluted by each one before he could get things under control.

By three o'clock in the afternoon, 11,500 people had paid their way into the theater, and the total for the first day's attendance was 21,000. Another thing about that first day which caused talk around the theater was this: The total for the day's sale at the candy counter was $900—which is some kind of a record, too.

BENNY GOODMAN
The Kingdom of Swing, 1939

In the last years of his life, illness slowed Louis Armstrong down and virtually ended his musical career. But on at least two occasions the brilliance of Armstrong's past was reawakened—at his seventieth birthday celebration in 1970, and at a nightclub appearance with Pearl Bailey. Jazz critic Leonard Feather, an admirer and friend of Armstrong's, was on hand both evenings and recorded the events that transpired.

Although tributes and celebrations had long since become his way of life, few if any were more important to Satch than the seventieth birthday celebration arranged by his old friend Floyd Levin, head of the Southern California Hot Jazz Society. Louis arrived at Los Angeles airport on the evening of June 30 and found, to his surprise, something he normally expected only at foreign airports: a big brass band, and hundreds of fans jamming the arrival area. Lucille [Mrs. Armstrong] did her best to whisk him away from the surging crowd and the Armstrongs left for their hotel after a brief press conference.

The concert was held at the Shrine Auditorium on the night of July 3, after a year of planning by a coalition of California Dixieland clubs. Almost 50 traditionalist jazzmen had been rounded up to represent various phases of the Satchmo story. I opened the proceedings by introducing the master of ceremonies, Hoagy Carmichael, who brought the guest of honor to the stage. At the sight of Louis, the crowd of 6,000 rose to its feet; the applause was as heartfelt and as long-lasting as one of Pops' high-C finales.

Seated in a rocking chair in front of a New Orleans French Quarter backdrop, Louis and Hoagy sang an unaccompanied duet—"Rockin' Chair," which they had recorded together in 1929. They then commented on a series of slides, which showed the wooden backyard building where Louis was born; thirteen-year-old Louis playing in the Waifs' Home band; the 1918 riverboat ensemble, and King Oliver's Creole band in 1923, with Louis on second cornet. As these reminders flashed on the screen, Louis reminisced freely while a succession of combos filed onstage to amplify his stories with music. (The riverboat band included, fittingly, many men who had been playing for years in a boat on a simulated Mississippi at Disneyland.)

Later, in a recreation of the Oliver band, Louis heard an old buddy, Andy Blakeney, who had replaced him with Oliver in 1924. The Armstrong Hot Five was represented by Teddy Buckner's group. Another combo, announced as the "Ambassador Satch Band," had four Armstrong alumni: Barney Bigard, Tyree Glenn, Joe Bushkin, and Red Callender.

As the midnight deadline approached, Louis reappeared to croak "Sleepy Time Down South," followed by "Blueberry Hill"; then he hypnotized the happy crowd into a sing-along, clap-along "Hello Dolly!" with Tyree Glenn up front playing the obbligato.

The evening was climaxed when an 800-pound cake, 11 feet high, was wheeled onstage. Satchmo had to climb up seven steps to take a slice off the top. In all it was a night filled with joy and love, in which the only missing element was the sound of Satchmo's horn. The question nagged at all of us: would he ever play again? "I still practice an hour a day, every evening before dinner," he told me. "Dr. Schiff says maybe I'll be ready in a couple of months."

Ready or not, his mere presence meant instant nostalgia to his fans. Everyone at the Shrine had his own private memory of Louis; perhaps a long-forgotten dance in a Depression-era ballroom; perhaps a forty-year-old Hot Five record that had triggered a career in music; perhaps the recollection of departed giants who had become part of the Armstrong legend—Joe Oliver, Jack Teagarden, Edmond Hall, Billy Kyle.

The next afternoon, on his actual birthday, Louis relaxed quietly with Tyree Glenn, Barney and Dorothe Bigard, Floyd Levin, and a few other friends in the sunlit penthouse apartment of Bobby Phillips of Associated Booking Corporation, the organization Joe Glaser had headed until his death.

Perhaps because Dr. Schiff was present, or perhaps because Louis wanted us all to know how seriously he took his doctor's injunction, he even refused to toot a note on a small toy trumpet that was handed him as a gag during the birthday party.

Looking back at the nostalgic joys of the previous evening, Louis turned to Levin and said: "Man, I've had a lot of wonderful honors in my life, but last night was the biggest thrill of all." So it had been for many of us whose pleasure was dimmed only by the belief that Louis had long since blown his final chorus.

As it turned out, the impossible took a little while. Two months later the International Hotel in Las Vegas announced: "The Pearl Bailey Show, with Louie Bellson and His Orchestra. Special Guest Attraction—Louis Armstrong." Pearl Bailey had the unprecedented pleasure of sharing her customary standing ovations with a legend brought back from limbo, and the overtones of this evening made it unforgettable.

It was not just Louis himself we applauded as he ambled onstage to the opening stanza of "Sleepy Time Down South"; it was the fact that he was once again able to play his horn, for the first time after two years of illness.

Satchmo and his combo (most of his 1968 men were back with him) cruised through their traditional show, with the usual "Indiana" for openers, followed by "Someday," "Tiger Rag," and "The Saints," among others. His horn had lost none of its incandescence. His sound might have been stronger, but we told ourselves that time would take care of that. Each note was perfectly on target and Armstrong-pure.

The teaming of Pearl and Louis was a delight as they traded choruses, from "Bill Bailey" to "Blueberry Hill." "Didn't We?" with occasional vocal murmurs from Satch, was Miss Bailey's most affecting ballad. For a finale the two of them went through a mutually stimulating series of choruses on "Exactly Like You." "There was an awful lot of love in the house tonight," Miss Bailey said later.

More than thirty-eight years had gone by since my first personal exposure to the Armstrong horn. It was just as well that nothing alerted me, during this evening of celebration, to the fact that this was, for me, the last time.

LEONARD FEATHER
From Satchmo to Miles, 1972

Mozart's Violin Sonata, K. 376

A Chronology of Music

Although song has probably always been a part of man's life, it is difficult to pinpoint dates in the history of music before the Middle Ages—and even then there are relatively few events that can accurately be cited. The reign of Pope Gregory I—Gregory the Great–from A.D. 590 to 604 saw the systemization of Church music, although it is not known how much Gregory himself had to do with the introduction of what came to be known as Gregorian chant. The Church continued to dominate music for another five hundred years—until the age of the troubadours saw the popularization of music and the development of a notation system that allowed men to record their songs permanently and accurately. Subsequently, composers, performers, and compositions can be listed in the long evolution of one of man's most important cultural expressions.

	1099	Soldiers of the First Crusade capture Jerusalem from the Moslems
Appearance of secular songs in Romance language (the dialect of southern France), written and performed by troubadours	1150-1200	
Leoninus of Notre Dame composes *Magnus Liber Organi*, series of musical pieces for the entire liturgical year	1160-1180	
	c.1168	Founding of Oxford University
	1183-1236	
Perotinus of Notre Dame perfects the four-part song	1194-1260	Western façade of Chartres cathedral constructed
	1215	Magna Carta signed by King John at Runnymede
Franco of Cologne explores the use of harmony in musical composition	1220	
"Sumer is icumen in," oldest English round	1226	
Stabat Mater, a part of Catholic liturgy, attributed to Jacopone da Todi	1228-1306	
Cantigas de Santa Maria produced at court of Alfonso the Wise of Castile	1250	
	1271-95	Journey of Marco Polo to the Orient
Life of Philippe de Vitry, theoretician and composer whose treatise *Ars Nova* ushered in a period of experimentation in musical composition	1291-1361	
	1321	Dante completes *The Divine Comedy*
Guillaume de Machaut, leading composer of the French *ars nova*, serves the royal house of France	1346-77	
Francesco Landino, the finest organist and composer of fourteenth-century Italy, wins a competition in Venice for organ compositions	1364	
	1368	Founding of the Ming dynasty, which ruled China for more than 200 years
	1415	Battle of Agincourt: English forces under Henry V defeat the French in a climactic battle of the Hundred Years' War
Guillaume Dufay composes *Sine nomine*, a Mass in three parts.	c.1420	
Dufay appointed conductor at the papal chapel	1428	
	1453	Fall of Constantinople to the Ottoman Turks
	c.1454	Publication of the Gutenberg Bible marks the beginning of printing from movable type
Josquin des Prés, master composer of medieval Church music, serves at papal court in Rome	1486-94	
	1492	Fall of Granada marks the end of Moorish influence in Spain; Christopher Columbus sets forth on his first voyage to the New World

Diversification of instruments: clavichord, virginal, spinet, harpsichord, violin, and lute come into common use	c.1500	
	1508	Michelangelo begins painting the ceiling of the Sistine Chapel
	1517	Martin Luther presents his "95 Theses"
	1519-22	Magellan circumnavigates the globe
	1543	Copernicus publishes his discoveries on the nature of the solar system
Book of Common Prayer, a Protestant hymn book, compiled by John Marbeck	1550	
Orlando di Lasso appointed chapelmaster at St. John Lateran in Rome	1553	
Palestrina composes *Missa Papae Marcelli* in honor of Pope Marcellus II	1565	
Giovanni Gabrieli named the organist of St. Mark's Basilica in Venice	1585	
English composer William Byrd publishes a volume of madrigals	1588	England turns back the Spanish Armada; Christopher Marlowe's *Dr. Faustus* performed
Publication of *Sacrae Symphoniae*, a collection of religious music composed by Gabrieli	1597	
More than 500 motets of Orlando di Lasso are published posthumously by his family	1604	Shakespeare's *Othello* first presented
Monteverdi's opera *Orfeo* performed in Mantua; employs first "modern" orchestra with more than 36 instruments	1607	
	1620	Pilgrims land at Plymouth Rock, Massachusetts
Samuel Scheidt writes *Tabulatura Nova*, the classic treatise on the art of organ music	1624	
Heinrich Schütz composes *Daphne*, the very earliest German opera	1627	
	1632	Galileo publishes his work supporting Copernicus' theories on the solar system, and the following year is tried for heresy by the Inquisition
	1642	Rembrandt completes his mammoth group portrait *The Night Watch*
Luigi Rossi produces *Orfeo*, the first Italian opera heard in Paris	1647	
	1666	Molière's comedy *Le Misanthrope* is performed
	1667	John Milton completes his epic poem *Paradise Lost*
Royal Academy of Music founded in Paris	1669	
Admission charged for the first time at a number of concerts held in London	1672	
Giovanni Battista Lully, considered the founder of French opera, directs the first performance of his *Alceste*	1674	
	1687	Isaac Newton publishes *Principia*, stating fundamental laws of gravity and motion
	1688	Glorious Revolution in England
Invention of the clarinet attributed to Johann Christoph Denner of Nüremberg	c.1690	
Francois Couperin becomes organist at Louis XIV's private chapel at Versailles	1693	
Alessandro Scarlatti becomes conductor at the chapel of the Polish court	1708	
Bartolomeo Cristofori develops modern pianoforte in which hammers are used to strike strings	1710	
Antonio Vivaldi composes the twelve concertos known as *Estro Armonico*	1712	
Handel writes *Te Deum* and *Jubilate* to celebrate the Peace of Utrecht	1713	Treaty of Utrecht
Violinist and composer Arcangelo Corelli composes the famous *Concerti Grossi*	1714	
Bach composes the six *Brandenburg Concertos*; one year later he completes the first volume of *The Well-Tempered Clavier*; second volume is published in 1740	1721	Publication of Montesquieu's *Lettres Persanes*

Production of John Gay's *The Beggar's Opera*	1727	
Bach's *The Passion According to Saint Matthew* is performed on Good Friday in Leipzig	1729	
Giovanni Pergolesi, a composer of religious and secular music, completes *Stabat Mater*	1736	Production of Voltaire's finest tragedy, *Zaire*
Royal Society of Musicians organized in London	1738	
First public performance of the English anthem "God Save the King"	1740	
Handel completes *Messiah*; the oratorio receives its first production the following year	1741	
	1758	Voltaire completes *Candide*
Haydn serves as *Kapellmeister* to the Esterházys	1760-90	
	1776	American Declaration of Independence; James Watt develops the steam engine; Adam Smith's classic treatise, *The Wealth of Nations*, published
First production of Mozart's *The Marriage of Figaro;* within the next five years Mozart completes *Don Giovanni, Così fan Tutte*, and *The Magic Flute*	1786	
In a three-month period Mozart composes three of his greatest symphonies: the E Flat, G Minor, and C, also known as the *Jupiter* symphony	1788	
	1789	Parisians storm the Bastille; Declaration of the Rights of Man proclaimed
French national anthem, "Le Marseillaise," is composed by Claude Rouget de Lisle	1792	
Paris Conservatory of Music opens	1795	
	1803	United States purchases Louisiana Territory
First performance of Beethoven's *Eroica* symphony	1804	
Beethoven completes the Fifth Symphony, perhaps the most popular piece of serious music ever written	1808	
Schubert writes the art song *Erl King*	1815	Napoleon defeated at Waterloo
Johann Maelzel invents the metronome	1816	
Beethoven composes his *Missa Solemnis*	1818-22	
Schubert completes Symphony No. 8 in B Minor, called the *Unfinished Symphony* because it has only two movements; Royal Academy of Music opens in London	1822	
Première performance of Beethoven's Ninth Symphony in Vienna	1824	First trade union formed in England
Mendelssohn composes *A Midsummer Night's Dream* overture; in 1843 he writes incidental music for a full-length production of the play	1826	
Initial performance of Hector Berlioz' *Symphonie fantastique*	1830	Victor Hugo writes *Notre-Dame de Paris*
Chopin settles in Paris	1831	
	1837	Accession of Queen Victoria of England
Robert Schumann writes *Dichterliebe*, a cycle of songs to poetry by Heine	1840	
New York Philharmonic Society and the Vienna Philharmonic are founded	1842	
Berlioz publishes *Treatise on Modern Instrumentation and Orchestration*, which becomes standard work on symphony orchestras	1844	
Johannes Brahms gives his first piano concert in Hamburg, Germany; publication of "Oh! Susanna," early work of American folk-music composer Stephen Foster; Franz Liszt appointed court conductor to the Grand Duke of Weimar; beginning of Liszt's friendship with Richard Wagner	1848	Revolutionary movements erupt and are quelled in Germany, Italy, Austria; abdication of Louis Philippe and proclamation of the Second Republic; Marx and Engels publish *Communist Manifesto*
	1850	Publication of Charles Dickens' *David Copperfield* and Nathaniel Hawthorne's *The Scarlet Letter*
Liszt composes *Sonata in B Minor*, considered the finest composition for the piano written in the romantic period; a year later he composes the symphonic poem *Les Préludes*	1853	
	1854	Commodore Perry secures agreements opening Japan to Western trade

	1859	Charles Darwin's *Origin of Species* . . . published
The Mighty Five—Russian composers Mili Balakirev, César Cui, Alexander Borodin, Nicholai Rimsky-Korsakov, and Modeste Moussorgsky—form a group dedicated to Russian national music	1862	
	1863	Battle of Gettysburg, turning point of American Civil War
Peter Ilich Tchaikovsky named professor of harmony at the Moscow Conservatory	1866	Fëdor Dostoevski's *Crime and Punishment* written
Johann Strauss the younger gives first performance of his own composition, *The Blue Danube Waltz*; Moussorgsky's *Night on Bald Mountain* performed	1867	
	1870-71	Franco-Prussian War ends with capitulation of Napoleon III and formation of Third Republic
"The Internationale," anthem of the international communist movement, written by the French composer Eugene Pottier; Verdi's *Aïda* receives initial performance in Egypt	1871	German Empire proclaimed; Otto von Bismarck becomes German chancellor
Smetana completes symphonic poems called *My Country*—best known of which is *The Moldau*	1874-79	
Johann Strauss the younger completes the popular operetta *Die Fledermaus*	1874	
Wagner's four-opera cycle *Der Ring des Nibelungen* presented at the first Bayreuth Festival; Tchaikovsky composes music for the ballet *Swan Lake*; Edvard Grieg writes *Peer Gynt Suites* as incidental music for the Ibsen play	1876	First telephone constructed by Alexander Graham Bell
Brahms scores his four symphonies—C Minor (1876), D Major (1877), F Major (1883), and E Minor (1885),—which rank among the most important orchestral works of the late nineteenth century	1876-85	
Gilbert and Sullivan's most popular operetta, *H.M.S. Pinafore*, presented in London	1878	Congress of Berlin convenes
	1879	Ibsen's *A Doll's House* performed
Rimsky-Korsakov composes the spectacular suite *Scheherazade*	1884	
Anton Bruckner, Wagner's disciple, writes *Te Deum*	1885	Louis Pasteur tests vaccine to prevent rabies
Cesar Franck's Symphony in D Minor performed	1889	
Tchaikovsky visits United States to participate in ceremonies marking the opening of Carnegie Hall	1891	
Antonin Dvorák leads the first performance of his Fifth Symphony, *From the New World*; Tchaikovsky completes his Sixth Symphony, called the *Pathétique*, and dies a few days after conducting its first performance	1893	
Claude Debussy, leader of the impressionist school of music. composes his most famous work, *L'Après-midi d'une Faun*	1894	Conviction of Dreyfus sparks controversy in France
Strauss writes the tone poem *Till Eulenspiegel's Merry Pranks; Also sprach Zarathustra* is produced a year later	1895	Publication of Freud's *Studies on Hysteria* marks beginning of psychoanalysis
Gustav Mahler heads Imperial Opera House, Vienna	1897-1907	
First performance of Sibelius' *Finlandia*; Symphony Hall in Boston opens	1900	Boxer Revolution in China crushed
Mahler conducts the first performance of his Third Symphony	1902	
Igor Stravinsky receives his first formal musical training as a pupil of Rimsky-Korsakov	1903	Orville and Wilbur Wright design and fly the first airplane
	1905-16	Albert Einstein formulates special and general theories of relativity
	1907	Pablo Picasso's *Les Demoiselles d'Avignon* exhibited
English composer Frederick Delius completes *In a Summer Garden*	1908	
Mahler serves as principal conductor of the New York Philharmonic	1909-10	
Gabriel Fauré completes the piano composition *Nine Préludes*	1910	Union of South Africa formed

Debut of Maurice Ravel's *Daphnis et Chloé* suite	1912	Chinese Republic proclaimed
Riotous uproar greets première performance of Stravinsky's *Le Sacre du Printemps* in Paris	1913	
	1913-28	Marcel Proust's multivolume masterpiece, *Remembrance of Things Past*, published
	1914	World War I begins; Panama Canal opens
	1917	Russian Revolution
Spanish composer Manuel de Falla writes the music for *The Three-Cornered-Hat* ballet	1919	
First performance of George Gershwin's *Rhapsody in Blue*; Arnold Schoenberg composes *Suite for Piano*, his first piece based entirely on the twelve-tone system; Arthur Honegger's *Pacific 231* has the orchestra imitating the sound of a steam locomotive; Respighi's *Pines of Rome*	1924	Sean O'Casey's *Juno and the Paycock* performed at Dublin's Abbey Playhouse
Duke Ellington organizes his first band; première performance of Aaron Copland's *Symphony for Organ and Orchestra*, commissioned by Nadia Boulanger for the New York Symphony Society	1925	
Ravel completes the popular symphonic piece *Boléro*	1928	Discovery of penicillin by Alexander Fleming
	1929	Stock market crash on Wall Street leads to worldwide economic depression
Première performance of Gershwin's *Porgy and Bess*	1935	
Sergei Prokofiev composes music to accompany the fairy tale *Peter and the Wolf*; Roy Harris' First Symphony performed	1936	Spanish Civil War begins
Dimitri Shostakovich writes the Fifth Symphony to celebrate the twentieth anniversary of the Bolshevik Revolution; Béla Bartók's *Music for String Instruments, Percussion and Celesta*	1937	
Charles Ives' *Second Piano Sonata*—written between 1904 and 1915—receives initial performance	1939	German invasion of Poland marks beginning of World War II
Paul Hindemith composes *The Four Temperaments*, theme and variations for piano and strings	1940	
Rodgers and Hammerstein's *Oklahoma!* sets a new style in American musical plays	1943	
Martha Graham choreographs an American folk ballet to Copland's *Appalachian Spring*	1944	
	1945	Allies defeat Hitler's Germany; first atomic bombs used against the Japanese to end World War II in Pacific; United Nations organized
	1947	India gains independence from Great Britain
	1948	State of Israel established
	1949	People's Republic of China proclaimed
	1950-52	Korean War
Canti di Liberazione by Luigi Dellapiccola	1951-55	
Karlheinz Stockhausen creates an electronic music composition, *Gesang der Junglinge*; opening of Lerner and Lowe's *My Fair Lady*	1956	First production of Eugene O'Neill's autobiographical play *Long Day's Journey Into Night*
Duke Ellington composes *Such Sweet Thunder*	1957	*Sputnik 1* launched by Soviet Union
French composer Pierre Boulez writes *Improvisation sur Mallarmé*	1958	Charles de Gaulle elected president of France; establishment of the Fifth Republic
Igor Stravinsky composes *Movements for Piano and Orchestra*—a major work of serial music	1960	
Benjamin Britten writes *War Requiem* to mark consecration of Coventry Cathedral in England; first United States tour of the Beatles	1962	Cuban missile crisis
	1963	Assassination of President John F. Kennedy
	1967	Arab-Israeli Six Day War; first heart transplant performed by Dr. Christiaan Barnard
Nearly half a million people gather for Woodstock rock festival in Bethel, New York; première of John Cage's multimedia composition *HPSCHD*	1969	American astronauts walk on the moon
Performance of Leonard Bernstein's *Mass* opens John F. Kennedy Center in Washington, D.C.	1972	
Seiji Ozawa becomes music director of the Boston Symphony Orchestra	1973	Agreement signed to end the Vietnam War

Selected Bibliography

Barzun, Jacques. *Berlioz and the Romantic Century*. 2 Vols. New York: Columbia University Press, 1969.

Briffault, Robert. *The Troubadours*. Bloomington: Indiana University Press, 1965.

Bukofzer, Manfred F. *Music in the Baroque Era*. New York: W. W. Norton, 1947.

Calvocoressi, M.D. and Abraham, Gerald. *Masters of Russian Music*. Reprint of 1936 edition. New York: Johnson Reprint Corporation.

Chase, Gilbert. *America's Music: From the Pilgrims to the Present*. New York: McGraw-Hill, 1955.

David, Hans T. and Mendel, Arthur, eds. *The Bach Reader*. New York: W. W. Norton, 1966.

Davison, Archibald T. and Apel, Willi, eds. *Historical Anthology of Music*. Cambridge: Harvard University Press, 1949.

Lockspeiser, Edward. *Debussy: His Life and Mind*. 2 Vols. New York: Macmillan, 1962.

Malm, William P. *Music Cultures of the Pacific Near East and Asia*. Englewood Cliffs: Prentice-Hall, 1967.

Newman, Ernest. *The Man Liszt*. New York: Taplinger, 1970.

Pleasants, Henry. *Serious Music and All That Jazz*. New York: Simon & Schuster, 1969.

Reese, Gustave. *Music in the Middle Ages*. New York: W. W. Norton, 1940.

Sachs, Curt. *The History of Musical Instruments*. New York: W. W. Norton, 1940.

———. *The Rise of Music in the Ancient World*. New York: W. W. Norton, 1943.

Schenk, Erich. *Mozart and His Times*. New York: Knopf, 1959.

Schindler, Anton F. *Beethoven As I Knew Him*. Edited by Donald W. MacArdle. New York: W. W. Norton, 1972.

Slonimsky, Nicolas. *Music Since 1900*. Fourth Ed. New York: Scribner's, 1971.

Stravinsky, Igor. *An Autobiography*. New York: W. W. Norton, 1962.

Strunk, Oliver, ed. *Source Readings in Music History*. New York: W. W. Norton, 1950.

Weinstock, Herbert. *Chopin*. New York: Knopf, 1949.

Wiora, Walter. *The Four Ages of Music*. Translated by M. Herter. New York: W. W. Norton, 1965.

Acknowledgments

The author, Mr. Grunfeld, wishes to express his special appreciation to the staffs of the British Museum library, and to the librarians of the Warburg Institute of London University, whose assistance was particularly helpful during the research phase of this book. Invaluable help in preparing the manuscript was provided by Barbara Barnes, Naomi Brandel, and Catherine Doggwiler.

Picture Credits

TITLE PAGE: Louvre, Paris (Lalance)

CHAPTER 1 **6** (Folco Quilici) **8-9** Instruments: Museo del Castello Sforzesco, Milan (Archives AME) **9** Bas-relief: Louvre, Paris (Foliot) **10** Wall painting: (Hirmer Fotoarchiv) **11** Ivory casket: Museo del Bargello, Florence (Scala) **12** New Delhi Museum (Borromeo) **13** Bibliothèque Nationale, Paris (Snark International) **14-15** Museo Nazionale, Naples (Parisio) **16-17** Antiquarium del Palatino, Rome **18** Museo Nazionale, Naples (Pedone) **19** Museo Lazaro, Madrid (Manso-Mas) **20-21** Both: Museo Archeologico Nazionale, Cividale del Friuli (Ciol)

CHAPTER 2 **22** Biblioteca Estense, Modena (Scala) **24-25** Palazzo Schifanoia, Ferrara (Arborio-Mella) **26** Jousting: Musée Condé, Chantilly (Snark International) Musicians: El Escorial (Molenaer) **27** El Escorial (Mas) **28** El Escorial (Molenaer) **29** Biblioteca Laurenziana, Florence (Scala) **30** Chartres: (Garanger-Giraudon) "Practica Musicae": Biblioteca Trivulziana, Milan **31** Biblioteca Civica,

Wagner: Museo Teatrale alla Scala, Milan **114** "The Wagnerians": Victoria and Albert Museum, London (Snark International) Johannes Brahms: Musées Municipaux, Carpentras (Bullox) **115** Oesterreichische Nationalbibliothek, Vienna

Index

okongo, 9–10
Oliver, Joe King, 144, 178
Ondine (Debussy), 122
Ondine (Ravel), 122
one-string guitar, 9–10
opera, 33, 36, 37, 45, 55, 96, 106–7, 108, 127
oratorio, 37, 55
Orfeo (Monteverdi), 37
organ, 21, 37, 43–45, 52, 124
organistra (hurdy-gurdies), 27
organum, 32–33
Origen, 19
Ormandy, Eugene, 175
Orpheus, 163, 164
Ospedale della Pietà, 41
Ottoboni, Cardinal, 54

Pacific 231 (Honnegger), 136
Paderewski, Ignaz, 170
Paganini, Nicolò, 92, 93, 100, 154
Paganini Etudes (Liszt), 102
Pagodes (Debussy), 118, 119
Palestrina, Giovanni Pierluigi da, 33, 36
Paris, 68, 91, 114, 117, 166–69
Paris Exhibition of 1889, 117, 119
Paris Industrial Exhibition of 1844, 97
Paris Opéra, 92
Parr, Andrée, 133
passacaglia, 20
Passion According to St. Matthew, The (Bach), 52
Paul, Eddie, 176
pavanes, 36
Pavillon d' Armide, Le (Diaghilev), 122
Peerce, Jan, 173
Pelléas et Mélisande (Debussy), 122, 123, 141
Perotinus, Master, 33
Persian lute, 10
Peters, Roberta, 174
Petrouchka (Stravinsky), 133, 136
Philadelphia Orchestra, 157–59
Philemon et Baucis (Haydn), 61
Philharmonic Academy of Bologna, 66–67
Philo of Alexandria, 19
piano, 21, 64, 77, 83, 86, 88, 92, 98–99, 101, 102, 136, 143
Piano Concerto, Opus 42 (Schoenberg), 139
Piano Concerto No. 1 (Tchaikovsky), 112
Piano Concerto No. 21 (Mozart), 72
Picasso, Pablo, 21, 132
piccolo, 124
Pinza, Ezio, 173
Piston, Walter, 169
pizzicato, 36
Plato, 15
Poème Electronique (Varèse), 140, 141
point *contra* point, 33
Poland, 92
polonaise, 99
Polonise in A-flat (Chopin), 165
polyphony, 30, 52
Polzelli, Loisa, 62

Pompadour, Madame de, 64
Pons, Lily, 174
Ponselle, Rosa, 173
pop music, 7, 26, 46, 143, 144, 151
Porgy and Bess (Gershwin), 145, 146, 147
postromanticism, 105, 137
Pourtalès, Countess de, 131
Power, Lionel, 33
Prague Symphony (Mozart), 73
Prelude, The (Wordsworth), 75
Preludes, Les (Liszt), 102
Preobrazhensky Guards, 108
Presley, Elvis, 143, 149
Prince Igor (Borodin), 108
Prokofiev, Sergei, 132, 161
Provence, 23
Prussian Academy of the Arts, 138
Psalsm, 19
psalteries, 27
psychoanalytic movement, 127
Puccini, Giacomo, 123
Puchberg, Michael, 73
Purcell, Henry, 40–41

Quartet in D Major for Strings (Tchaikovsky), 112

Radicati, Felix, 79
raga, 12, 15, 32
raga-mala, 12
Rake's Progress, The, 136
Rameau, Jean Philippe, 33, 40
ranz-des-vaches (tune), 98
Rapsodie espagnole (Ravell), 119
Rasoumovsky Quartets (Beethoven), 79
Ravel, Maurice, 119–24, 131, 149, 167
rebab, 118
rebec, 27
Recio, Marie, 93
recorder, 11, 27
Red and the Black, The (Stendhal), 91
Reik, Theodore, 127
Reiner, Fritz, 173
Reinken, Adam, 45
Renaissance, 24, 28, 33, 91
Requiem (Verdi), 172
Requiem Mass (Berlioz), 96
Rhapsody in Blue (Gershwin), 145, 175
Ride of the Valkyries (Wagner), 158
Rigaud, Francis, 62
Riley, Terry, 143
Rimsky-Korsakov, Nikolai, 105, 107, 108, 117, 136
Ringling Brothers and Barnum & Bailey Circus, 137
rock (music), 143
rock 'n roll, 149
"Rockin Chair," 177
Rodgers, Richard, 173
Rolling Stones, 143
romanticism, 72, 75, 82, 83, 87, 91–99, 100–103, 105
Romberg, Sigmund, 173
Rome, 15, 18
Romeo and Juliet (Berlioz), 96
Romeo and Juliet (Shakespeare), 92

Rore, Cipriano de, 36
Rosenkavalier, Der (Strauss), 126, 127
Rossini, Gioacchino, 100
Rouen Cathedral, 32
round dance, 18
Rubenstein, Anton, 165
Rubinstein, Arthur, 21, 164–66, 173, 174
Russian guitar, 8

Sacre du Printemps, Le (Stravinsky), 131–32, 133, 136, 137
"Saints, The," 179
Salome (Strauss), 127
Salome (Wilde), 126
Salomon, Johann Peter, 62
Salzburg, Prince-archbishop of, 64
Sand, George, 91, 98, 99–100, 102
Sandoval, Miguel, 174
Santo Domingo de Silos, monastery of, 20
Saora tribe, 8–9
Saraswathi (Hindu goddess), 10
Sargeant, Winthrop, 154–57
Saul (Handel), 55
Sayn-Wittgenstein, Princess Carolyn, 102
Scarlatti, Domenico, 52, 53, 54, 55
Scheel, Fritz, 157, 165, 166
scherzo, 99
Schiele, Egon, 127
Schiller, Friedrich, 75
Schindler, Anton, 89
Schlictegroll, Heinrich von, 73
Schoenberg, Arnold, 115, 123, 124, 137–40
Scholes, Percy, 133
Schöne Müllerin, Die (Schubert), 88, 89
Schubert, Franz, 86–89, 145, 151
Schuller, Arthur, 174
Schumann, Robert, 45, 83, 86, 101, 102, 103
Schütz, Heinrich, 37
Schwärmerei, 81
Scythian Suite (Prokofiev), 132
Sebastian, John, 173
Sehnsucht, 98
selumpret, 118
"Sergeant Pepper," 151
Seville, Moorish court of, 28
Shakespeare, William, 36, 83, 92, 93, 173
Shankar, Ravi, 143
Shapero, Harold, 169
shawm, 27
Shéhérazade (Ravel), 122
"She's a Woman," 150–51
Sibelius, Jean, 112, 129
side drum, 124
Silberman, Gottfried, 46
Sinatra, Frank, 149, 173
sinfonia, 41
sirens, 136
sirventés, 25
sitar, 10–12, 32, 143, 151
Sitwell, Sacheverell, 63
Six, Les, 132–36
Six Bagatelles for String Quartet (Webern), 140